Divided by the Bounty

Alan Adams

© 2010 Alan Adams
Divided by the Bounty

ISBN 978-0-9567732-0-3

Published by
Bounty Publications
7 Garden Court
Garden Close
Shoreham-by-Sea
West Sussex BN43 6BS

The right of Alan Adams to be identified as the author of this work has been asserted by him in accordance with the Copyright, Designs and Patents Act 1988.

A CIP catalogue record of this book
can be obtained from the British Library.

Book designed by Michael Walsh at
THE BETTER BOOK COMPANY
5 Lime Close, Chichester PO19 6SW

and printed by
IMPRINTDIGITAL.NET
Seychelles Farm, Upton Pyne, Exeter Devon EX5 5HY

Divided by the Bounty
Alan Adams

Acknowledgements:-
Hackney Archives
Thames River Police
National Maritime Museum
National Archives London
Guildhall Library London
London Metropolitan Archives
Tower Hamlets Local History Library
State Library of Massachusetts U.S.A.
Mitchell Library Sydney Australia

Front cover adapted by David Ransom:- HMS Bounty in Darling Harbour, Sydney. Reconstruction used in 1984 movie 'The Bounty' featuring Mel Gibson and Anthony Hopkins

alanadams@supanet.com

Basic Adams Family Tree

[1] Jonathan Adams [b.?-d.l748] m. Rachell Williams
Collar maker, Allhallows, Tottenham, 1726

|

[2] John Adams [1731-1783] m?Dinah [?-d.1774]
Bargeman, St. John at Hackney

|

[3] Jonathan [1774-1842] Dinah Jemima [b.1757] Rachel [b.1754] John [b.1767-1829]
Waterman, St. John at Hackney
m. Margaret Mouncey [b.1778]   Seaman and Bounty Mutineer
St. Mary's, Rotherhithe 1794

| |

[4] John Adams [b.1803-1870]   PITCAIRN ISLAND
Thames River Policeman, St.George in the East   Vahineatua   Teio
m. Mary Park 1823, St.Anne's Limehouse

| Dinah   Rachel Hannah   George
             [b.1796] [b.1797] [b.1799] [b.1804 d.1873]

[5] Francis Jonathan Adams [b.1837-d.1918]
Lighterman, St.George in the East   NORFOLK ISLAND
m. Elizabeth Beasley [b. ? - d.1872]   m. Polly Young [b.1796-d.1843]
St. Philip's, Bethnal Green 1859

| John Adams [b.1827-d.1897]
                  m. Caroline Quintal [b.1827]

[6] John Adams [b. 1861-d. 1930]   Jonathan Adams [b.1829-d.1906]
Carman, St.George in the East   m. Phoebe Quintal [b.1824]
m. Mary Ann Riley [b. ?-1942] 1890   Josiah Chester Adams [b. 1830-d. 1907]
St. Mary's, Spital Square, Spitalfields   m. Diana McCoy [b.1838]

|

[7] Francis Adams [b.1892-d.1933]
Carman/newsvendor. Mile End Old Town
m. Alice Dye [b.1894-d.1978]
St. Paul's, Bethnal Green 1913

|

[8] Francis Adams [b.1914-d.1958]
Labourer, London Hospital,Whitechapel
m. Alice Catherine Simmonds [b.1917-d.1988]
St. Thomas's, Bethnal Green, 1937

|

[9] Alan Adams b.1946 Bethnal Green

FATE OF THE BOUNTY'S CREW

WILLIAM BLIGH, Lieutenant aged 33. Captain of the Bounty. Retired as Vice Admiral of the Blue. Died aged 64, 1817.

JOHN FRYER Master aged 33. Survived launch voyage to Timor Further service in Royal Navy.Died 1817

WILLIAM COLE. Boatswain. Joined Bligh in Launch. Returned safely to England.

WILLIAM PECKOVER. Gunner. Previous service with Captain Cook. Joined launch. Returned safely to England

WILLIAM PURCELL. Carpenter. Survived launch voyage. Last surviving crew member, died 1834.

THOMAS HUGGAN. Surgeon Drank himself to death on the voyage toTahiti.

THOMAS LEDWARD. Surgeon's mate. Survived the launch voyage to Timor. Drowned on the way back to England

FLETCHER CHRISTIAN. Master's Mate Aged 22. Leader of Mutiny. Killed by natives on Pitcairn, 1793.

WILLIAM ELPHINSTONE. Master's Mate, aged 36. Survived launch voyage but died in Batavia, 1789.

JOHN HALLET. Midshipman. Aged 15. Survived launch voyage. Returned to Tahiti on the ill-fated Pandora in 1791.

THOMAS HAYWARD. Midshipman. Aged 20. Survived launch voyage and joined Pandora searching for mutineers.

PETER HEYWOOD. Midshipman. Aged 15. Captured on Tahiti and found guilty of mutiny. Later pardoned. Died 1831.

ROBERT TINKLER. Midshipman. Aged 17. Survived launch voyage. Rose to Post Captain.

EDWARD YOUNG. Midshipman. Aged 21. Mutineer. Died of lung disease on Pitcairn Island in 1800.

GEORGE STEWART. Midshipman. Aged 21. Captured on Tahiti. Drowned in the wreck of HMS Pandora.

PETER LINKLETTER. Quartermaster. Aged 30. Survived the launch voyage but died in Batavia.

JOHN NORTON. Quartermaster. Aged 34. Joined Bligh in the launch. Murdered in Tofua.

GEORGE SIMPSON. Quartermaster's mate. Aged 27. Survived launch voyage. Returned to England.

JAMES MORRISON. Boatswain's Mate. Aged 27. Captured, sentenced to death but later pardoned. Died 1807.

JOHN MILLS. Gunner's mate. Aged 39. Mutineer. Killed by natives on Pitcairn, l793.

CHARLES NORMAN. Carpenter's mate.Aged 24. Captured on Tahiti. Acquitted of mutiny in 1792.

THOMAS McINTOSH Carpenter's mate. Aged 25. Captured on Tahiti. Acquitted of mutiny in 1792.

LAWRENCE LEBOGUE. Sailmaker. Aged 40.Survived launch voyage. Sailed on second breadfruit voyage.

JOSEPH COLEMAN. Armourer. Aged 36. Captured on Tahiti. Acquitted of mutiny in 1792.

CHARLES CHURCHILL. Corporal. Aged 28. Murdered on return to Tahiti in 1790.

HENRY HILLBRANT. Cooper. Aged 24. Captured in Tahiti. Drowned in the wreck of the Pandora.

WILLIAM MUSPRAT. Steward. Aged 27. Captured on Tahiti. Found guilty but discharged on technicality.

JOHN SAMUEL. Clerk. Aged 26. Survived launch voyage and promoted to Paymaster on return.

THOMAS HALL. Ship's cook. Aged 38. Survived launch voyage but died in Batavia.

JOHN SMITH. Commander's cook. Aged 36. Survived launch voyage. Sailed on second breadfruit voyage.

ROBERT LAMB. Butcher. Aged 21 Survived launch voyage But died on way back to England.

RICHARD SKINNER. Able Seaman. Captured on Tahiti. Died in the wreck of the Pandora, 1791.

ALEX. SMITH, [JOHN ADAMS] Aged 20. Last surviving mutineer on Pitcairn. Died aged 62 in 1829.

THOMAS BURKITT. Aged 25. Able Seaman. Captured on Tahiti. Found guilty and hanged in 1792.

JOHN MILLWARD.Aged 21. Able Seaman. Captured on Tahiti. Found guilty and hanged in 1792

JOHN WILLIAMS. Aged 26. Able Seaman. Settled on Pitcairn with mutineers. Killed,1793.

JOHN SUMNER. Aged 22. Able Seaman. Captured on Tahiti. Drowned in the wreck of the Pandora, 1792.

MATTHEW THOMPSON. Aged 37. Able Seaman. Killed by natives in Tahiti, 1790.

JAMES VALENTINE. Aged 28 Able Seaman. Died of blood poisoning before Tahiti, 1788.

MICHAEL BYRNE. Aged 26. Able seaman and musician. Acquitted at the court martial.

WILLIAM McCOY. Aged 23. Fell or pushed off cliff on Pitcairn whilst drunk 1799.

MATTHEW QUINTAL Aged 21. Able Seaman. Killed by Adams and Young, 1799.

ISAAC MARTIN. Aged 30. Able Seaman. Killed by natives on Pitcairn, 1793.

THOMAS ELLISON. Aged 19. Able Seaman. Convicted mutineer. Hanged in 1792.

DAVID NELSON. Gardener. Survived launch voyage. Died of fever in Coupang, 1789.

WILLIAM BROWN. Aged 25. Gardener's assistant.Killed by by natives on Pitcairn, 1793.

Index

Researching the past

Some twenty years ago driven by sudden curiosity to find out about my origins I decided to trace my family history. By this time previous generations, including parents and grandparents, had all passed away with their primary source of knowledge, which led to the realisation that I knew hardly anything about them. My paternal grandmother, born in Hoxton, Alice Adams née Dye [1894-1978], lived long enough for me to know, but as a younger person I regretfully never had much interest in the past. A regret that genealogists are familiar with once relatives have passed on.

Alice Dye, although born and bred in the East End of London, perhaps unknown to her, had roots before 1850 in Norfolk. Her family were in the furniture trade as cabinet makers and French polishers. At the time the Hoxton and Shoreditch area was the centre of the industry and I think the move to London was for economic reasons. Her father Adam Alfred Dye when he died was an undertaker, and with the earlier death of her mother left Alice an orphan at ten years old to be brought up by older siblings. Through my researches I've realised since she must have had a really tough life, becoming a widow for over forty years and losing her sister and seven members of her family in one night during the Blitz. However my memory of her is one of always being happy and positive, a characteristic of East Enders at the time. So, with little background knowledge to work from, I painstakingly set out on a voyage of discovery of the roots of my Adams predecessors and found much more than I could have imagined at the start.

Tracing backwards through birth, marriage and death records, censuses and parish records, I gradually began to piece together a family tree. In the early 1990s interest in genealogy was minimal and before the availability of computers, the internet, family history centres etc. a much more difficult undertaking. Record offices at the time were often cramped with indifferent heating and air conditioning as in many government institutions situated in old buildings. However, we should be grateful for the wealth of records that have survived, been retained and are now much more accessible. There is quite a lot on-line available to the searcher, helpful as a first stop, but for me the pleasure is in finding the original source material.

Some information transcribed can be very useful but can also be inaccurate and misleading. Original records can also, sometimes, be set down wrongly, and where possible clues should be confirmed from another source, which in some cases can lead to more information.

To track back to 1837 when registration of births, marriages and deaths began to be recorded by the government it is fairly straightforward, providing your ancestors were informing the authorities which was not always the case. Before that date, parish records must be searched.

We owe the keeping of parish records to the Tudor period, as prior to that such information was not regarded as important. It was introduced by Thomas Cromwell, chief minister to the King in 1538. With Henry VIII's split from the Church of Rome and the practice of Roman Catholicism, or any other religion being made illegal, the keeping of parish records was a way of confirming a family's loyalty to the King and the Church of England by registering their baptisms, marriages and burials in the local church. Also useful are the 10 yearly censuses starting in 1841, but with no disclosures until a census is 100 years old.

Understanding these records can be subject to the handwriting of the individual scribe and can vary from being beautifully written or a scrawl, perhaps depending on the writer or the sharpness of his quill pen. The earliest Adams ancestor I have been able to find with any certainty is my Gt. Grandfather [x6] married in 1726. Before that the records are poor, incomplete, perhaps in Latin and difficult to verify.

As more records come to light you begin to realise the terrible existence many of our ancestors had to endure with war, disease and famine and early deaths commonplace. With little in the way of relief for the unemployed, sick, poor and needy, every day was a constant struggle just to get by. Infant mortality was high and it was not unexpected if a child died before five years of age. Diseases such as the plague, which had wiped out much of Europe in years gone by, were thankfully a rarity by the 19th century but smallpox, scarlet fever, cholera, typhoid, tuberculosis and other ailments mostly had little or no prevention or cure.

I see today's generations as the product of the fortunate survivors of their ancestors that lived long enough to have descendants and continue the line of descent.

By 1800 the population of England and Wales was around eight million with one million living in the London area. So, a much smaller haystack to find the needles in than today for the genealogist, but with less available and reliable information the further you go back.

Prior to the industrial revolution and the invention of the railway with poor roads, families were less transient in the 18th century. Most people would usually be found not far from their home parish, as it would offer a basic local support network in times of strife and hardship depending on long term residency of their parish. Most couples married and settled within a small radius of either spouse's home parish, usually the husband's, where his wife and children would assume the same settlement rights. This was to prove to be an important factor in my family before the end of the 18th century. England was made up mostly of small towns and villages, with a third of the population in 1800 involved in agriculture but by 1900 this was reduced to about ten per cent, as vast numbers migrated to the industrial towns and cities seeking work in the mills and factories.

Starting the search

Once the search is underway there is always the faint hope of an ancestor, famous or infamous, to put on the family tree. Some people researching their roots set out to prove or disprove family rumours as well as discovering their forebears. In my case I had virtually a blank sheet and little in the way of documents which seemed to have disappeared along with old family photographs. However from this poor start I made good progress over many years when time allowed, and discovered most of my ancestors, like me, were from the east side of London.

I've found many people of interest and a few skeletons in the closet, but as George Bernard Shaw said 'If you cannot get rid of the family skeleton you may as well make it dance'.

For the most part they were decent hardworking people involved through the Adams line, all in what is now Greater London, frequently on the River Thames as watermen, lightermen, river policemen and others as diverse as carmen, firemen, beadles and also in the East End furniture trade. However, I found a few exceptions to the norm, such as a 'suicide whilst lunatic, a philanderer with four 'wives' and at least twelve children, an over-keen police officer, a WWI absconder and a Royal Navy mutineer and murderer. The suicidal lunatic plays an important part in early events and, to my best knowledge, the tragic circumstances of his death have never been revealed before and must have had an effect on what was to follow.

The philanderer, Francis Jonathan Adams [1837-1918] was described as a 'Bluebeard' in a family rumour, from a distant cousin, whose grandfather had met him. I am a descendant of his second son [John Adams born 1861] from his first legal marriage in 1859. This first wife, Catherine Elizabeth Beasley after having five children, died young from 'abortion convulsions' in 1872. The cousin is from his second 'wife" Adelaide Godin, although she took the Adams name, no wedding or marriage documents have been found to date. It's possible she may have been of foreign extraction with the surname of Godin, which may be French or Huguenot, as there were many in East London at the time, in the silk weaving trade. She also died young in 1879 from peritonitis after having three children.

During the relationship with 'wife' number three, Frances Cox, again no marriage documents, they lived in the Spitalfields/Whitechapel area, in Heneage St., at the time of the Jack the Ripper murders in 1888.

A recent TV documentary, using the latest forensics and profiling attempted to establish the identity of the Ripper and stated that the murderer probably lived in that surrounding area. Flower and Dean Street was pinpointed which is just a couple of streets away from Heneage Street, off Brick Lane, Whitechapel. By the next year, after the last killing, great grandfather had left the East End for Sunderland with a new baby and wife number four, Jane Dorothy Brown, this one legal, leaving behind 'wife' number three and twelve children aged between twenty eight and three and he was not to return for fifteen years. Could this obvious ladies' man have been a Ripper suspect, or did he just move away to find work as a lighterman, as this was the year of the London Dock strike? I don't suppose we'll ever know!

The police officer [John Adams 1803-1870] was a member of the Thames River Police from 1826-1856 and he was reprimanded more than once for attending court on his days off and improperly interfering in cases presumably to intimidate witnesses and defendants to secure convictions. He managed to hang on to his job and after thirty years service he was retired with a pension of £39 per annum. He later worked as a Beadle for the Tower Liberty to supplement his income from his pension.

From ancient times the Liberties were virtually autonomous districts with their own gaol and courthouse set up around the Tower of London for its protection, but by the mid Victorian period they had started to lose their powers. A Beadle was employed mostly on church vestry business but may have assisted the local constable with keeping order in the locality.

The WWI absconder [Francis Adams 1892-1933] after returning home wounded from the Somme went temporarily absent without leave on a few occasions but always returned after a short time. Looking at it from a 21st century perspective, I can see no shame or dishonour. Who could blame a married man with a child [my father] looking for some respite after being sent overseas to take part in that madness? He was sentenced to eight months in a military prison and then shipped out, after a reduced sentence, under guard to Salonika. After a year he caught malaria, rampant in the area at the time, and was hospitalised before being shipped home. His final punishment, once fit, was to be sent to Germany in 1919, long after the war was over, to look after prisoners-of-war. Back in England he absconded for the last time, but the authorities, after being unable to find his whereabouts, decided to discharge him eventually in September 1919.

The last character was John Adams [1767-1829] able seaman and mutineer on the ill-fated HMS Bounty breadfruit voyage to Tahiti under Captain Bligh. John was the only brother of my Gt. Grand-father [x4] Jonathan Adams [1774- 1842]. With the sailing of the Bounty from Deptford in 1787 the lives of John [aged 20] and of brother Jonathan [aged 13], left behind were to take entirely differ-ent paths and to lead to a separation of the two sides of the family for almost 220 years.

After the mutiny, John and the other mutineers and their newly acquired partners, settled on the tiny and remote island of Pitcairn in the South Pacific. It was there, after much turmoil, that he was forced to murder one of his few fellow remaining deserters and to establish the settlement that survives to the present day.

Jonathan was to live, work, raise a family and die in the East End of London where descendants, through to my generation, remained. All this was yet to be discovered at the beginning with no prior knowledge. It was to be at least 8 years from the outset before fate took a hand in my discovery of the Bounty connection, leading me to uncover previously unknown facts about the brothers' humble past and their lives after their parting in 1787.

What follows is an investigation into the life and times of the Adams family from John and Jonathan's grandparents in 1727 up to their grandchildren over a period of around 150 years.

Bounty connections

Everybody has some knowledge of the story of the Mutiny on the Bounty through films, books and even a musical on the 200th anniversary in 1989 but I'm not sure if it is seen as a true event and is certainly not always correctly portrayed. The last film to be made in 1983 starring Mel Gibson as Fletcher Christian and Anthony Hopkins as William Bligh called 'The Bounty' often strays from the truth. The John Adams portrayal, as one instance, shows him as a middle-aged man from the north of England when in fact he was only twenty years old and from London. Also at that time he was known as Alexander Smith yet was referred to as Adams several times in the film. Just one of several parts of the story to differ from reality.

Most people know the two main characters William Bligh, and his adversary, Fletcher Christian, but members of the crew are not so recognisable in what is still regarded today as one the most infamous incidents in the history of the Royal Navy.

As the two main protagonists came from old established families their lineage is quite well documented. Of the rest of the crew of 44 [including not only sailors but a surgeon and mate, and a botanist and his assistant taken on board to tend to the breadfruit plants] there are only scant details of their origins and descendants. All who sailed were volunteers, none press-ganged, but of the original number that signed on; one was discharged, two were transferred and fifteen deserted before leaving England.

One important factor, unusual for the time, was no marines were taken due to restrictions in space and to keep costs down. They were normally enlisted to enforce order and discipline on ships, perhaps a mistake by the organisers of the voyage, not expecting trouble and short of funding. Maybe with them the outcome of the voyage may have been different.

Countless fine books, articles and documentaries have been produced over the last 200 years about the Mutiny, but to my knowledge no in-depth investigations of many of the crew's families, backgrounds or circumstances prior to signing on and their later fates has been undertaken.

The aim of this story is to portray the life before and after the event of one of them, Able Seaman John Adams, and to contrast that with his brother Jonathan, left behind and never to meet again. I have obtained details of the life in Hackney, then a rural village on the north-eastern edge of London, including details of the considerable local history of the area. Information gathered includes their grandparents' marriage, their grandfather's and father's occupations and their wives and the brothers' two sisters. Both parents died early [the father a suicidal lunatic] making the family dependent on the parish, leaving the boys in the workhouse aged 6 and 13, and to the start of the vastly diverse lives they were to lead as a result.

I will outline only briefly the details of the mutiny as there are plenty of good references elsewhere with coverage in more detail and much speculation. With my research I've tried to produce as much documentation as possible to back up the information that follows. Where educated guesses are given I have stated so. Before the story of the Mutiny on the Bounty and what happened before and after, I will explain my chance connection to it.

About 8 years into tracing my family history and slowly working backwards I eventually reached my Gt. Grandfather [x3], John Adams born in 1803. His father on the baptism register at St. George in the East, Stepney in East London was given as Jonathan Adams, waterman, mother Margaret, living in Knight's Court, Wapping. His job as a Master Waterman was to transport passengers and their goods up, down and across the River Thames at a time when many journeys by boat in the capital would have been quicker than by road.

It was a highly regulated and skilful trade requiring an apprenticeship of seven years before achieving 'freedom'. There were set fares and a good standard of behaviour expected, or the offender would be punished after being identified by the numbered badge on their arm and boat. However it was a tough business, out in all weathers, on a polluted River Thames. They were noted for their coarse language and frequently fined for various misdemeanours.

Jonathan gained his 'freedom' from seven years apprenticeship in 1796 aged 21 and plied his trade originally from Union Stairs and later Wapping New Stairs, close to his home in Knight's Court. These allocated plying places or 'stairs' were so called as they were steps leading down to the water's edge for embarkation whether it was a low or a high tide. There were many of these along both banks of the Thames some of which can still be seen today. Soon after having arrived at this stage in my research serendipity played a part, and, as sometimes is the case, something that I may have found mildly interesting just weeks before became a startling revelation.

I picked up a booklet in Tower Hamlets Local History Library entitled 'Captain Bligh in Wapping' by Madge Darby. Because of the recently discovered Wapping connection and an interest in Captain Cook, who married a Wapping innkeeper's daughter [The Bell near Execution Dock], and, who I later found out, Bligh had sailed with on his last fateful voyage I decided to buy it. On reading it, I was amazed to find on the very last page that John Adams, a mutineer on the Bounty, had a brother Jonathan, a waterman, who had lived in Upper Gun Alley, Wapping and their last meeting was at Deptford prior to sailing on the ill-fated breadfruit voyage to Tahiti under William Bligh. Of course this was all news to me as I had only just recently found out about his brother Jonathan.

The name of John Adams, or as I found out later the name he used when signing on, Alexander Smith, is rarely mentioned in the films or dramas and so I was not at all aware of a possible family connection. Could it really be true that he was my Gt. Uncle [x4] ?

Intent on finding out more about the Mutiny on the Bounty, I discovered there is a copy on microfilm of the Bounty log at the National Archives in Kew. After much searching and checking the crew list, I could find no reference to an Adams on board, even amongst those that had signed on, but never turned up for whatever reason. Disappointed and confused by this, I decided to check reference books at the library to try to make some sense of it. From only having a brief knowledge, like most people, of the event I researched a number of books and several accounts and it soon became clear to me that Bligh and his crew never knew John Adams by that name. For various reasons, not uncommon at the time, many sailors would sign on under a false name. The name chosen was Alexander Smith, on which I will speculate later, his real name not emerging for twenty years.

Bligh in Wapping

Captain William Bligh, An engraving by A.J. Conde Courtesy of the National Maritime Museum

Bligh whilst living in Wapping in Broad St. [1785-1790] with his wife and children, undertook the task to sail to Tahiti on the breadfruit voyage after lean years with the Royal Navy.

A vastly experienced officer, brilliant navigator and hydrographer, he sailed with Cook on his last voyage to the South Pacific as a sailing master. He was admired by his senior officers but not always getting the full credit for the charting of their discoveries. Several other Wapping men were to sail with Bligh to Tahiti, including William Peckover, gunner, who after sailing on all three of Cook's South Seas expeditions was one of the most travelled sailors of his time.

When Cook was killed on Hawaii in 1779, Bligh, due to the illness of senior officers, had to assume responsibility for HM ships Resolution and Discovery and see them home. In more fortunate circumstances, on his return he may have been seen as a natural successor to Cook and achieved the promotions he craved. Although a skilled and proven officer, at the end of the American War of Independence there was little work for seafaring men and he was put on half pay. Anxious to get back to sea, through his wife's family he was able to secure work in the merchant trade to the West Indies. It was on these voyages that he first met and befriended Fletcher Christian who pleaded to sail under the man who had served under Captain Cook. Christian had turned to the navy at the unusually late age of eighteen after financial problems had beset the family, and being the fourth son it left little money for pursuing further education or another career. Bligh, however, initially refused Christian's parents request, claiming a full complement. This prompted Fletcher to write back saying "Wages are no object: I only wish to learn my profession, and if you would permit me to mess with the gentlemen, I will readily enter your ship as a foremaster, until there be a vacancy among the officers." Bligh relented and set in motion a chain of events that was to have far reaching consequences. Respect and friendship grew between the two men over two voyages to the West Indies, Christian first serving as a gunner and then as second mate but, it was not to last. The Royal Navy paid much less than the merchant trade but as an ambitious man to finally achieve the rank of Captain, to enhance his pay and status, Bligh accepted the Bounty commission. However, although captain of the ship he remained a lieutenant for the breadfruit voyage and with such a small crew of just 45, was left with only a few junior officers and no marines.

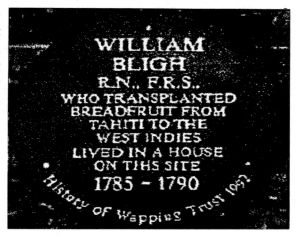

Blue plaque on old London Dock Wall, Broad Street, Wapping.

WILLIAM BLIGH R.N., F.R.S., WHO TRANSPLANTED BREADFRUIT FROM TAHITI TO THE WEST INDIES LIVED IN A HOUSE ON THIS SITE 1785 - 1790

History of Wapping Trust 1992

William Bligh in Sydney, Australia

18th Century Wapping

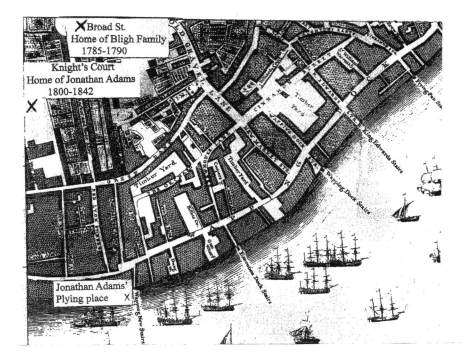

Wapping

The name of Wapping originates from the Saxon settlement of Waeppa's people, also known as Wapping in the Wose or Wash. Until development and drainage of the marshland was undertaken it remained a rural area, but over time from a small village and due to its proximity to the River Thames it became of more importance by the 16th century as an anchorage for the increasing amount of shipping coming upriver into London.

Wapping, at the end of the 18th century was very much a sailor town with many taverns, ship's chandlers, boat builders and mast makers, warehouses and victuallers' stores strung out along the dockside and Wapping High Street with alleyways leading off. The area was bordered to the north by the ancient track known as The Highway, to the south by the River Thames, east by Shadwell and west by the Tower of London. A good place to find work if you were a seaman or beware of the press gang if you had no wish to go to sea. In the 16th century the historian John Stow described Wapping as "a continual street, or a filthy strait passage, with alleys of small tenements or cottages built, inhabited by sailor's victuallers." It could be a dark and dangerous place best avoided if possible.

The population and building expanded over the next 300 years to accommodate the booming trade in shipping and the building of the docks to serve London, the busiest port in the world. However, it remained as it does today, with most of the maritime industry now gone, a backwater island, in the East End of London, formed by the docks and accessed by bridges. Much of the docklands was destroyed in the Blitz but there are still some buildings such as the 16th century Prospect of Whitby [originally known as the Devil's Tavern]. It is said to be the oldest riverside pub in London and the scene of cockfighting and bare knuckle boxing in earlier times and visited by the likes of Pepys, Dickens and Turner and many famous people before and since. In the early 17th century a sailor returning from the West Indies sold a beautiful plant, not seen before in England, to a local market gardener for a measure of rum in the Prospect of Whitby. From this was developed the popular fuchsia we know today. The Town of Ramsgate pub [named after the Ramsgate fishermen that unloaded their catch on the stairs alongside] is on the site of a 16th century tavern and said to be where 'hanging judge Jeffries' of the Bloody Assizes was captured before fleeing abroad when things started to go wrong. He condemned over 300 men to the gallows and watched them hang at Execution Dock from nearby taverns and was also responsible for another 800 transported. He fell out of favour with the King and became a wanted man, and whilst trying to escape was recognised by a former victim in the pub, was captured and sent to the Tower of London where he eventually died through drink.

Captain Blood, stealer of the Crown Jewels and conspirator against Charles 11 was arrested at the bar of this pub in 1671, so it is claimed. The extensive cellars under the pub were used as a prison for convicts awaiting their transportation to the colonies and also for victims of the press gang. Wapping Old Stairs alongside the Town of Ramsgate is believed to be the site of Execution Dock where pirates, including Captain Kidd, met their fate. The last hangings, always well attended, were in 1830.

The oldest police force in the world was established in 1798 at Wapping New Stairs to deter crime along the river and waterfront. The Thames Division today occupies the police station built in 1908 on the site of the first building. There are few old pubs now compared with years gone by when there was at least thirty just along the High Street in its heyday. Other buildings to have survived are the Georgian Pierhead houses built in 1813 for senior dock officials at either side of the entrance to the original London Docks, now filled in, and are well preserved. St. John's church built in 1756 but heavily damaged in the Blitz and used by the Adams family in the 18/19th centuries has only the original tower and graveyard left and has been converted into apartments. Unfortunately the homes of William Bligh in Broad St. and Jonathan Adams were lost with the building of the London Docks.

Above: Town of Ramsgate pub adjacent to this alleyway leading to Wapping Old Stairs.

Opposite page top: Wapping Old Stairs. Across the river can be seen the spire of St. Mary's Rotherhithe where Jonathan Adams was married.

Opposite page below: Thames River Police Station on the same site over 200 years

Above:

The Georgian Pierhead houses above were built in 1813 for dock officials either side of London Dock entrance, now filled in and almost covered by trees. In the middle distance can be seen the spire of St. George in the East, the Adams; parish church in the 19th century.

St John's Parish Church Wapping

The Bounty mission

There are many aspects to the Bounty saga, apart from the act of the mutiny. Other elements are, the hazardous outward leg of the journey, life on the paradise island of Tahiti and relationships formed there, Bligh's epic sailing of a packed open boat to Timor, the tragic sinking of the Pandora returning some of the mutineers to England, and the flight of the rest to escape execution and find a safe refuge. There are many references to -all these incidences from many other sources. In view of this, I will just give an outline of events and concentrate on how this affected the lives of John and Jonathan Adams, the circumstances leading up to their parting and subsequent fortunes.

The Bounty, originally the 'Bethia' was commissioned by the Royal Navy under the guidance of Sir Joseph Banks the noted botanist, and backed by King George III. Banks had sailed with Captain Cook and was aware of the flora of the South Pacific. He knew of the breadfruit plant growing plentifully in the South Seas from his explorations with Cook, and that it was a useful source of food. The owners of the sugar plantations in the West Indies were looking for an alternative source of food from bananas to feed the slaves and as Tahiti has a similar climate to those islands it was thought the breadfruit would be an ideal cheap supplement. Bligh's mission was to remove samples of the plant, transport them to the West Indies to see if they would flourish there, as a viable and inexpensive alternative food source.

The 'Bethia', a small, flat-bottomed coastal cutter just 91 feet long, was purchased from her owners Wellbank, Sharp and Brown for £1950 and fitted out at a cost of £4456 to carry 1000 breadfruit saplings. This type of ship, similar to the ones used by Captain Cook, was originally used to transport coal from N.E. England and due to its flat bottom it could be beached, if necessary, for loading, unloading or repairs. Quite useful in remote areas of the world where there may not be ports or docking facilities. There was little spare room even with a crew of just forty-six, but was deemed adequate for the task. The Bounty carried some weapons but was not heavily armed and none of the men were press ganged, as with such a small complement, willing experienced sailors were needed.

For the necessary work to be done, she was taken to Deptford Dockyard in S.E. London to be fitted out as a floating greenhouse and to allow for the maximum number of breadfruit plants, even to the extent of Bligh giving up the captain's cabin for one much smaller.

The figurehead, at the front of the ship, chosen was a lady in a riding habit. Below decks, living for the crew would have been unpleasant, claustrophobic and almost completely dark. The ship was now officially renamed the 'HMAV Bounty' [His Majesty's Armed Vessel].

As the senior officer of the ship, Bligh was the captain but in rank still just a lieutenant, although a successful voyage would count in his favour for a much desired promotion on his return.

Fitted out and provisioned for a mission to the far side of the world, HMAV Bounty left Deptford for Portsmouth to await favourable winds to set out for Tahiti.

John Adams [signed on as Alexander Smith] was listed as an able seaman probably indicating previous experience at sea. He and his brother Jonathan are said to have made their farewells on the deck of the Bounty before she left the London dockyard and, unknowingly, never to meet again. A separation of the two sides of the family which was to last until the 21st century.

After arriving at Portsmouth it was to be some time before the Bounty was able to leave its anchorage at Spithead waiting for suitable tides and weather to carry the ship through the English Channel. They were finally underway on the 23rd December, 1787. The late departure was to have dire consequences later during the voyage.

The Outward Journey

Although a harsh taskmaster, short-tempered, foul-mouthed and abusive to the point of being offensive, Bligh was no worse than many captains of that era, when it was essential to maintain discipline on board ship. After these flare-ups he would soon calm down and, as these apparently frequently occurred in the morning, it has led to conjecture that he may have had hangovers and a drink problem, but this has not been proved. He states in his log he was hoping to accomplish the mission without punishing anyone. He looked after the welfare and fitness of the crew by insisting on a diet to avoid scurvy, and exercising by compulsory dancing to a half-blind fiddler taken aboard especially for that purpose. He also changed the normal watch from two to three, so for every four hours worked eight hours were taken off, apart from emergencies. There were few disciplinary problems on the way out, although the doctor soon became ineffective as he was drinking himself to death. The shortest way to Tahiti using the trade winds was by way of the Canary Islands and Rio de Janeiro, and around the southern tip of South America, the notorious Cape Horn. Because of the delayed start, adverse weather conditions had now set in, and after battling away for several weeks and making no headway around Tierra del Fuego, off Cape Horn, reluctantly Bligh was forced to turn about and head east for Cape Town on the southern tip of South Africa and then by way of Tasmania reaching Tahiti later than hoped for.

On arriving at the safe anchorage of Matavai Bay the ship received a warm welcome from the Tahitian natives who regarded white men as friends. The stay on Tahiti was longer than expected, either due to the breadfruit season being over or, some say waiting for favourable weather to set off again. Either way, there was to be a delay of 5 months, which left the crew with little to do on an island paradise with plenty of food and drink and friendly, uninhibited native women. A recipe for trouble to come.

Above: Breadfruit tree.   Below: Tahitian Breadfruit

Monument at Point Venus. Matavai Bay in background

Storm clouds over Matavai Bay's safe anchorage

Point Venus

Tahiti

A visitor to Tahiti today, now part of French Polynesia, may get the impression that the British had no influence on the island as the French have left few mentions of the time the Royal Navy spent there. In fact the first European to visit was a British ship's captain called Samuel Wallis of HMS Dolphin in 1767 who named it King George's Island. He arrived home in time to advise the Royal Society who were organising an expedition to measure the transit of Venus across the Sun and that Tahiti would be ideal for that purpose. James Cook, on HMS *Endeavour*, was chosen and sent to Tahiti in 1769 to carry out this task from the north of the island, adjacent to the safe anchorage of Matavai Bay at a location now named Point Venus. This was a rare event, only twice seen in a hundred years, and was carried out from a fort specially built for protection from the natives, and the steadiness of the instruments. The data recorded would enable scientists to calculate the distance from the Earth to the Sun and used as a unit for measuring the Universe. Cook earned the respect of the Tahitians by showing compassion and understanding and was treated god-like.

Less than a year after Wallis, the Frenchman Bougainvilla, who gave his name to the shrub, arrived followed by others including William Bligh, once with Cook and twice to collect breadfruit.

By the time the plants were gathered, most of the crew, including Fletcher Christian, but not Bligh, had formed relationships with native women and got used to the relaxed life of the island, many sailors being heavily tattooed Polynesian style like the Tahitians.

This was far removed from the tough existence of a sailor with the hardships and poor quality of life many of the crew had come from in England. Three deserters on the island hoping to stay behind when captured, were only flogged, one with 12 lashes of the cat-of nine tails and the other two 24 lashes, repeated later, when they could have been hanged. With such a small crew, Bligh was probably wary of losing too many men. Alexander Smith [John Adams] was also flogged, according to the Bounty log, for losing a metal gudgeon, part of the large cutter's rudder. This was stolen by the natives, who were unfamiliar with metal until the arrival of the Europeans and it was highly valued by them. Some of the crew sought favours from the native women by offering nails from the Bounty planks. This had to be stopped before it became serious.

Smith was given 12 lashes, when 5 0 to 100 was not unusual at the time. Because the natives were expert swimmers, a closer watch was kept around the Bounty and the cutter and the punishment was probably a warning to the crew to be on their guard.

Entry in the Bounty Log:-

> '*Several petty thefts having been committed by the natives owing to the negligence and inattention of the petty officers and men, which has always tended to alarm the chiefs. I was under the necessity this afternoon to punish* **Alex Smith** *with 12 lashes for suffering the gudgeon of the large cutter to be drawn out without knowing it. Several chiefs were on board at the time, and with their wives interceded on behalf of the man, but seeing it had no effect they retired and the women in general showed every degree of sympathy which marked them to be the most humane and affectionate creatures in the world.*'

At last, after some five months the Bounty, now fully laden with breadfruit plants, set sail on 5th April 1789; fifteen months after leaving England. With hardly any time at sea during the 23 weeks on Tahiti, it was probably a mistake by Bligh not to keep the crew ready to begin the journey to the West Indies, and ill discipline and discord had set in about leaving new made friends and relationships. It wasn't to be very long before discontent was felt amongst the men, for various reasons well documented elsewhere, but mostly believed to be the leaving of Tahiti and the personality clash between Bligh and Christian. Events came to a head on 28th April 1789.

Mutiny

In my opinion, Bligh has been harshly treated by history and I believe him to be no worse, and better than some in the treatment of his crew. I think it was the weakness of Fletcher Christian, unable to bear the brunt of Bligh's tirades that stirred unrest among some of the men already wishing to be back to the idyllic life on Tahiti. According to Bligh's logbook Alexander Smith [John Adams] played an active part being armed and standing guard over him, before Bligh and some of the loyal crew were put in the longboat. More wished to go, but as it was dangerously low in the water it was not possible to fit them all in. Later, some of these unfortunate sailors, although they had not wanted to go along with the mutineers back to Tahiti, were to be treated as such and taken back to England to stand trial.

Entry in the Bounty log on the day of the mutiny:-

> *'Just before sunrise Mr Christian, Mate, Chas Churchill, Ship's corporal, John Mills Gunner's mate and Thomas Burkitt, Seaman, came into my Cabbin while I was asleep and seizing me tyed my hands with a cord behind my back and threatened me with instant death if I spoke or made the least noise. I however cried so loud as to alarm everyone but the officers found themselves secured by sentinels at their doors. There were four men in my Cabbin and three outside, viz **Alex Smith**, Jn. Sumner and Mat Quintal. Mr. Christian had a cutlass in his had the other had musquets and bayonets. I was forced on deck in my shirt suffering great pain from the violence with which they had tied my hands. I demanded the reason for such a violent act but I received no answer but threats of instant death if I did not hold my tongue ..."*

The longboat was cut adrift with scant supplies, enough thought by the mutineers to enable the loyal crew to reach one of the many islands in that area of the South Pacific, but giving plenty of time to make their escape. However, Bligh had other ideas, anxious to get back to England and report the loss of his ship to 'pirates', he decided to sail to the nearest port he knew he could be sure of getting a passage back home. Against all the odds, by superb seamanship and discipline in adverse conditions, little food and water and unfriendly natives, killing one of his men, they managed to reach

Timor in the Dutch East Indies, a journey of 4000 miles in 43 days, one of the greatest open boat voyages in history. After securing a passage home, Bligh returned to England to face a court martial to explain the serious offence of losing his ship.

Although in a dire situation Bligh still managed to chart their course and set down physical descriptions of the mutineers in his log –

> *Fletcher Christian age 24 Master's Mate 5ft 9ins high. Blackish or very dark brown complexion Dark Brown hair ... strong made. A star tatowed on his left breast and tatowed on the backside. His knees stand a little out and he may be called a little Bow Legged. He is subject to violent perspiration, particularly in his hands so that he soils anything he handles ...*

> *Alexr. Smith Age 22 ab ...5ft 5ins high, Brown Complexion, Brown Hair, Strong Made – much pitted with the smallpox and very much tatowed on his Body, Legs, Arms and Feet and has scar on his Right Foot where he has been cut with a Wood Axe ...'*

From this description it is not hard to imagine that John Adams [Alexander Smith] had had a difficult early life. Smallpox, known as the 'Speckled Monster' was the scourge of the 18th century when prevention by inoculation and vaccination was in its infancy. Edward Jenner's discovery of vaccination with the cow pox virus, from observing milk maids avoidance of the smallpox, was to be more widely used towards the end of the century.

Most died from this dreaded disease or could be left blinded or disfigured if they survived. First symptoms were increasing red spots all over the body, building up pus behind them, after a few days mouth membranes swelling, leading to delirium, the victim becoming unrecognisable and eventually to suffocation. After eleven to twelve days, should the sufferer still be alive the pustules would dry up, flake off and leave permanent scarring, but at least would have survived. Far from being shunned, these survivors would be employable, as once they had smallpox they would not bring it to an area or workplace having already had it. John Adams was seven years old in 1774 when his mother, Dinah, died; perhaps struck down by the 'Speckled Monster' at the same time as her son, but not surviving. Unfortunately, the burial record at St. John at Hackney, gives no indication of cause of death. As for the cut by a wood axe, which must have been extremely painful and dangerous prior to antiseptic treatments of wounds, that may have been as a result of his daily chores as a young man in Hackney or time as a sailor. His young life, overcoming disease, injury and loss of both parents must have built up his character and determination, which was to stand him in good stead during later years.

Of the 19 men set adrift in the longboat only 12 were to reach England safely, dying from the journey and disease. Bligh finally reached Portsmouth on 13th March 1790 eleven months after losing his ship. He had to explain himself to the Admiralty for the serious circumstances that had befallen him.

Back on the Bounty, once the breadfruit plants were thrown overboard a decision had to be made about what to do next, knowing they would be hunted by the Royal Navy, although unaware that Bligh had made it back to England.

By studying Blights charts, Christian decided Toobouai, an island 350 miles south of Tahiti, would be a suitable refuge. After a brief visit to the island, discovered by Cook but never landed on, a decision was made to permanently stay there but first returning to Tahiti, to replenish stores. Once arriving on Toobouai it was soon evident the natives, unlike the Tahitians, were far from friendly and blood was spilt when the natives attempted to take the ship.

In spite of this, Christian insisted it was the right place to settle once they picked up their female partners and others from Tahiti, along with necessary livestock and goods. At this time every sailor not set adrift in Bligh's boat, but had wanted no part in the mutiny, were still aboard the Bounty. Christian persuaded all the crew when they arrived back in Matavai Bay in Tahiti, just nine weeks after leaving, it was not safe to remain and after stocking with hundreds of pigs, goats, fowl and cats and dogs and an assortment of natives they returned to Toobouai.

The attempt to establish a colony there was doomed from the start when, after negotiations with one island chief for land, the new arrivals found a more desirable plot elsewhere from another chief. There were also arguments over the stealing of their women and the hundreds of pigs let loose to run free, causing considerable damage to the islanders crops. It was felt necessary to build some form of defensive encampment with 12ft high walls and a wide ditch, and cannons on the walls patriotically calling it Fort George, and proudly flying the Union Jack. Ill feeling ran high between the sailors and the native Toobouains and it became difficult to leave the fort to hunt or fish or to tend to their agriculture. On one occasion John Adams was captured and kept overnight, leading to speculation as to how future events would have panned out if he had been killed. Christian decided to go on the offensive and in the ensuing battle sixty-six native Toobouains were killed, but no losses from the Bounty party. After this, the time had come to dismast the Bounty and strip anything useful from it if they were to stay. After two and half months, with unrest and discontent among the sailors and further hostilities likely, it was decided to return to Tahiti and for the loyalists to have the opportunity to stay if they so desired.

There they could await the certain arrival of a Royal Navy ship which would surely come to look for the mutineers.

Back in Matavai Bay, Tahiti, it was agreed that Christian and his followers could take the ship, but there would be a fair division of the stores, alcohol, arms and ammunition. Once done, the Bounty slipped away in late September 1789, with nine mutineers and an assortment of six native men and twelve women and a baby, to seek another refuge.

HMS Pandora

The ill-fated Pandora was sent in 1790 under the notorious Captain Edward Edwards, assisted by midshipman Thomas Hayward, one of the original Bounty crew and a Bligh loyalist, to capture the mutineers of the Bounty. Edwards, by reputation, was known as a harsher captain than Bligh; perhaps the reason he was chosen. He immediately proved that on his arrival in Tahiti. After capturing all the crew left by Christian he incarcerated guilty and innocent alike on the return journey to England that it was never to complete sinking off the Australian coast.

Captain Edwards arrived on Tahiti and soon sought out the stranded seamen, many of the loyal crew unable to go with Bligh thinking they were rescued. However all of Bounty's crew, loyal or mutineer, on the island were rounded up, put in chains and imprisoned in "Pandora's Box", a purpose built cell with little light or ventilation on the quarterdeck. This was later to prove tragic for some when she ran aground and sank off the Great Barrier Reef. Thirty-one of the ship's company and four captives from Tahiti, two still in irons, were lost but the Captain survived. His severe treatment of the prisoners continued even after the shipwreck. On finding a beach to find some respite they were denied shelter from the blazing sun and had to bury themselves in the sand to prevent sunstroke. Edwards eventually managed to reach Coupang in Timor, like Bligh, and return to England.

Captain Edwards was cleared of all negligence by a court martial, although it was the third ship lost under his command. He was never to take to sea again and became a land based Admiral.

The Life of William Bligh {1754-1817}

The names Fletcher Christian and William Bligh are forever linked to the infamous act of the Mutiny on the Bounty. For Bligh, it was just one sad chapter in a life filled with triumph and disaster throughout his naval career. Christian, the product of an old established Manx family from the Isle of Man, with a privileged upbringing, is known for little else during his short life. His life and influence after the mutiny and their arrival on Pitcairn Island was to be shortlived in contrast to Bligh who, remaining controversial was to go on to have a distinguished career serving his country.

William Bligh was born in St.Tudy in Cornwall in 1754, the son of a customs official in Plymouth, and was destined for a naval career from an early age. The custom at the time was to sign on very young men, seven years old in William's case, to show years of service to assist in rapid promotion. In reality most would not serve until much older but would be seen on the books as having acquired several years at sea and therefore officer material. However, when he eventually went to sea he was taken on only as an Able Seaman until a midshipman's vacancy was available. Within six years, in 1776, he had achieved the rank of Sailing Master and selected for the third expedition to the South Seas with the legendary Captain Cook. This was to be the last fatal voyage for Cook when he was killed by natives on Hawaii. Bligh's exceptional navigational and mapping skills helped to get the fleet home where he was required to report and give details of the expedition. With the end of the American War of Independence and a reduced navy, Bligh, on half pay was forced to take work for a while in the merchant trade through contacts of his wife's family. Although more lucrative he longed to return to the Royal Navy, being very ambitious to further his career and promotion. By the time he was offered the Breadfruit Voyage in 1787 he had served on many ships at different ranks, merchant and Royal Navy, for seventeen years.

He was to have a career of over forty years but was constantly noticed throughout to be rude, offensive, arrogant and not a sufferer of people he deemed to be fools.

Back in England after the mutiny and his epic open boat voyage William Bligh was given a hero's welcome. He was rewarded with 500 guineas for his valiant efforts to take breadfruit to the West Indies. Feted by the public, nobility and royalty alike he wrote a best selling book of his trials. However, at this time his version of events was the only one available until the return and trial of the captured mutineers being sought by Captain Edward Edwards of the ill-fated 'Pandora.' Before their return it was decided Bligh needed to complete his mission and a second breadfruit voyage was undertaken, and as a newly promoted Captain, this time completed successfully. He was rewarded with a further 1000 guineas.

During his absence, however, the stranded Bounty crew were taken back from Tahiti, guilty and innocent treated the same, by Captain Edwards. All those that returned to England were survivors of the sinking of the 'Pandora' sunk off the Australian coast and eventually stood trial.

Facts now emerged to show Bligh in a poor light particularly his lies about young Peter Heywood. Bligh's allegations about complicity in the mutiny by Heywood were testified by the rest of the crew not to be true. He was acquitted with a Royal Pardon, although there were later suspicions that he was not totally innocent. If Bligh had had his way this intelligent young man, compiler of a Polynesian dictionary whilst on Tahiti, who went on to serve in the Royal Navy for over 40 years, would have been swinging from the yardarm along with three convicted mutineers.

The Heywood and Christian families campaigned to show Bligh as a tyrant, a bully, offensive and an irrational leader of men. This exposure undermined all the positive things about Bligh as an excellent sailor, not one to punish excessively and a captain who looked after the health, fitness and cleanliness of his ship and men. As a result of this he was left ashore, out of favour, for the following two years after the second breadfruit voyage.

Bligh was to be involved in two other mutinies during his career, though neither was of his making.

With hostilities against the Dutch, French and the Danes at the end of the 18th century, he was needed and given command of a ship once again. When the Nore fleet mutinied for the removal of unpopular officers and better treatment of crews, he was not alone in being removed from his ship and escaped any reprimand this time.

His undoubted seamanship and bravery was to enhance his reputation, particularly at the Battle of Copenhagen, after which he was publicly thanked by Horatio Nelson for his courage against the Danish flagship in their victory. Bligh did not seem to mellow over the years, constantly being reported for openly berating fellow officers and men under his command. For persistently coming to the attention of the naval authorities, Bligh was deemed not suitable for the Channel Fleet keeping Napoleon at bay.

Sir Joseph Banks, his mentor from the breadfruit voyages and with Cook made him an offer of the Governorship of the penal colony of New South Wales in Australia. He accepted the challenge, although it meant leaving his wife and family behind for four years, but perhaps a chance to make his fortune. True to form, on the outward journey he fell foul of the captain of the fleet, arrogantly defying his orders and disputing the commander's actions. Once in Sydney the roles were reversed and as Governor, still bearing a grudge, he was in overall charge. In a show of spite, he ordered the fleet commander to immediately return to England, taking his wife and family but leaving his possessions behind. The return journey, so soon after arriving, in an old leaking boat, proved to be too arduous and the commander's wife and child died, but Bligh was acquitted of any wrongdoing.

The third mutiny was during his governorship of New South Wales centred around the so called 'Rum Rebellion.' Bligh attempted to control the traffic in illicit spirit in the colony, but due to his lack of manpower to enforce regulations he was overpowered and arrested. By a strange coincidence the supplier of the spirit into Australia was said to be the Yankee sealer 'Topaz' later to discover the mutineers on Pitcairn Island, in 1808, on its return journey to America.

Bligh returned to England in 1810 for the court-martial of Major George Johnston, the leader of the Rum Rebellion, but was no doubt glad to get back to his family after a long separation. Soon after, he was promoted to Rear Admiral and finished his service as Vice Admiral of the Blue.

He retired to Lambeth in South London and lived at 100, Lambeth Road opposite the new Bethlehem Royal Hospital lunatic asylum known as Bedlam and what is now the Imperial War Museum. In 1817, he is said to have dropped dead in Bond Street on a visit from his later home in Kent. I have found no comment from Bligh on the fate of the escaped mutineers, by then common knowledge, but he must have had some satisfaction knowing that the only survivor was John Adams.

Tinten Manor Farmhouse, St.Tudy
Birthplace of William Bligh,1754

100, Lambeth Road, London
Bligh's home after the mutiny

Moorland Close, Cockermouth, Cumbria
Birthplace of Fletcher Christian, 1764

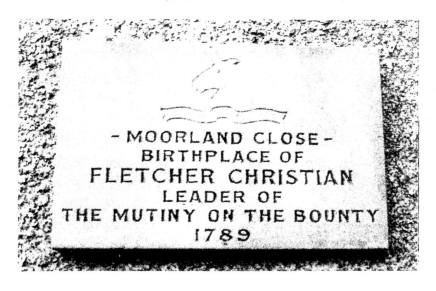

The Unicorn is depicted in the Manx Family crest.
Family motto – 'Salus per Christum' – 'Savation through Christ'

William Bligh's tomb in St Mary's church, Lambeth

The tomb is made from Coade stone, a product widely used in the 18th and 19th centuries. The local factory was in Narrow Wall, Lambeth, run by a widow, Mrs Coade, and her daughter.

It was a moulded artificial stone material but unlike concrete. It is a type of ceramic fired at very high temperatures to give a hard surface finish.

The inscription reads:

SACRED

To the memory of

WILLIAM BLIGH esq. FRS

Vice Admiral of the Blue

The celebrated navigator

Who first transplated the Breadfruit Tree

From Otaheite to the West Indies

Bravely fought the battles of his country

And died beloved, respected and lamented

On the 7th day of December 1817, aged 64.

Pitcairn Island

The Bounty left Tahiti for the last time in their quest for a new refuge, sailing with a much reduced crew having just two watches instead of Bligh's three. During the long search it was noticed that an island named Pitcairn's Island, after the British sailor first to spot it in 1767, was not where it was shown on the map. By keeping on the same latitude for some 200 miles it was eventually found but wrongly charted on the Royal Navy maps and so could be the haven they were looking for. The choice of this secluded island {measuring only one mile by two and mostly steep) was to turn out to be very advantageous, mainly avoided by other shipping due to the inability to land safely with precipitous cliffs and raging currents, and so it proved as there was to be no visitors for twenty years.

Pitcairn was no longer inhabited, although there were signs of previous occupations in the past, but nothing permanent left and was probably just visited by itinerant South Sea Islanders. Although landing was, and still is hazardous, it was achieved with no major problems. It was soon evident that there would be sufficient food and water already available on the island, and trees for building, with fish in the surrounding sea. Enough for the small band of fugitives' survival.

All useful items were removed from the Bounty and, fearing discovery from passing ships noticing habitation on the island, she was set on fire and destroyed and the dogs killed for fear that their barking may attract unwanted attention.

Much was to happen in the ensuing years, before Captain Folger in 1808 of the American ship Topaz became the first visitor to find only John Adams left of the original mutineers and native men.

Fletcher Christian's role after the mutiny was to be short-lived, unlike John Adams forming a long standing community on Pitcairn, and William Bligh after the initial embarrassment of losing his ship, who went on to forge a successful career in the Royal Navy.

Origins

In contrast to John Adams now isolated forever on Pitcairn Island, his only brother, Jonathan, in the year of the mutiny had begun an apprenticeship as a waterman on the River Thames in London, in Wapping. At the early stages of my research an area I falsely assumed they both came from. John Adams attempted to write about his early life but left scant clues. However with some evidence from correspondence, after decades of separation, between them and a useful document from the State Library of Massachusetts I've been able to piece together their early years.

The brothers, by 1790, were now on opposite sides of the world, John on Pitcairn Island and Jonathan in Wapping, beginning his own career, never realising it was to be a permanent separation.

As far as I am aware there are scant biographies about the background of the fellow mutineers of John Adams. A Jonathan Adams was known to be the brother of John but until I made it known I was a direct relation very little information was available about what had become of him.

The lives of Bligh and Christian are quite well documented as they both came from prominent families. Fletcher Christian's family, originally from Cumberland and later the Isle of Man, especially .were of a higher status than Bligh's, from Devon, perhaps something else that rankled with him. Of the ordinary able seamen there is a general outline of age, birthplace and physical descriptions but not of their parentage or siblings. For the descendants of the mutineers on Pitcairn Island and later on Norfolk Island I am grateful to PJ Lareau for sending me a copy of the excellent 'HMS Bounty Genealogies' which continues up till today and fills in some of the blanks.

What follows is how I've researched as far back as possible with any certainty to discover the early lives of the brothers and their siblings, parents and grandparents, the times and the place they lived in with their unusual connections and a tragedy so early in their childhood. After that I will return to their separation and the different paths each had taken over the remainder of their lives.

To recap then, in my genealogical research I had reached as far back as my Gt. Grandfather {x3} Jonathan Adams, aged 16 in 1790 and working as an apprentice waterman on the River Thames at Wapping. By this time news of the mutiny had reached England, whether or not Jonathan knew of the link to Alexander Smith or how it may have affected him I suppose we'll never know.

After the revelation about John Adams of the Bounty, I assumed at this stage in my research they had both originated from the London dockland area, as they were both involved with working on the water.

However, it was fortunate that there had been some correspondence after 30 years between Pitcairn Island and Wapping and it became known that John Adams had attempted to write down his early life, which although only brief, throws some light on their home parish of St. John at Hackney, which was then on the rural outskirts of North East London.

The original document for this is part of a journal started by Matthew Quintal setting down his early life in the West Country and his first experiences at sea. The journal is an old English blank book of approximately 100 pages, each 16x10 inches, of which only twelve pages have handwriting, and have an English watermark dating it to around the end of the 18th century.

Apart from the background information on Quintal and Adams it contains the birthdates of Quintal's children, Tahitian words and their translation and a newspaper clipping from an American newspaper dated 1881. The book must have come from the Bounty and Quintal's entries written before his brutal death in 1799. John Adams was known to have given souvenirs from the Bounty to visitors to Pitcairn Island. It is believed that he gave the journal to Captain Reynolds of the 'Sultan', an American ship out of Boston. In turn it was given to the New England Museum and then belonged to Daniel Seagrove of Worcester before ending up in the State Library of Massachusetts where it resides in their digital collection today. Very few pages have anything written on them but they give a valuable insight into the background of Quintal and Adams. Although in poor condition after all its travels the writing is mostly quite legible.

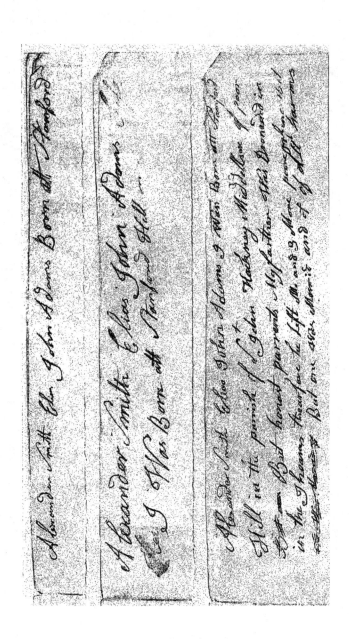

*Extract from Matthew Quintal's Journal from Pitcairn Island
Courtesy of State Library of Massachusetts*

Two pages from the journal of Matthew Quintal [Quintrell] telling
his early life and some Tahitian/English translations.
Courtesy of the State Library of Massachusetts Digital Collections

The three attempts in his own words and handwriting giving a few clues to his early life is as follows:-

"I was born at Stanford Hill in the parish of St John at Hackney Middellsex of poor but honast parents. My farther was drouned in the Theames therefore he left me and 3 poore orfing but one was married and out of all harmes way"; stated John Adams. In another instance he wrote "The life of John Adams, born 5th November in the year 66. My farther was sarvent to Daniel Bell cole marchant. My father was drowned in the River Theames" {sic}. A check of the parish records at St. John at Hackney soon proved the baptism of a John Adams in 1767 and a brother Jonathan baptised in 1774. There were also 2 sisters, Rachel baptised 1754 and Dinah Jemima baptised 1757. The parents are stated as John and Dinah Adams. The same names were used constantly as was the custom in those days for generations which can make tracing the family line sometimes easier if the names are not too commonplace.

So much of what John had written was true but doesn't tell the whole sad story of the loss of their parents and the circumstances and consequences that followed. More of that to come later.

Jonathan received word from his brother, probably long presumed dead, after 30 years. By this time ships were stopping at Pitcairn Island more frequently after many years of isolation.

In 1818 a correspondent {T.W} to the Gentlemen's Magazine writes to say he contacted Jonathan in Wapping and asked for him to visit as he had news of his brother. The article states that Jonathan was now working as a waterman and was also a retained fireman for an insurance company {before the later formation of The London Fire Brigade}. His part-time employment was with The London Assurance and he was stated to be a steady character who proudly wore his firecoat and armband. T.W suggested if he would like to write a letter to John he had the means to transmit it to him. He also mentioned that perhaps Jonathan would allow his eldest son, Andrew aged 21, to go out to Pitcairn Island. This was rejected referring to "the influence Dolly had with John Bull" intimating his mother would be against it.

The letter was sent on 4th November 1818 and Captain Henderson of the Hercules delivered it to Pitcairn on 18th January 1819. It contained details of Jonathan's work and family, the death of one sister and the prosperity of the other. The news affected John Adams {now using his real name) very deeply; often repeating he never expected to see this day or any of his countrymen again.

His reply stated "My dear brother, I this day have the greatest pleasure in my life since I left my native country that is of receiving your letter, dated 13th October 1818.

I have now lived on the island 30 years and have a wife and 4 children and considering the occasion which brought me here it is not likely I shall ever leave this place. I enjoy good health and except the wound which I received from one of the Otaheitians when they quarrelled with us have not had a day's sickness.

Wishing you every health and happiness this world can afford you, I remain, my dear brother, your affectionate brother, John Adams".

Stamford Hill, Parish of St John at Hackney

From this information I was able to gather more information of their earlier life and continue my search through my family history. Without the attempt by John Adams to set down his young life, it would have been difficult to make the connection between Wapping by the River Thames, and Stamford Hill to the Northeast, roughly 6 miles away, a considerable distance in those days. Now part of Greater London, Stamford Hill, at the time that the family lived there during the 18th century, was little more than a hamlet and a rural community on the furthest reaches of St. John at Hackney parish.

Situated on the main road north to Cambridge, the original Roman road called Ermine St {now the A 10} passes through Stamford Hill and it was also a part of a Pilgrim's route to Waltham Abbey. The road ran across the higher ground of Stamford Hill to avoid flooding from the River Lea nearby, and thereby keeping the main road open for travellers. Early references show it was called Sanford Hill, probably due to a sandy ford over Hackney Brook. By the end of the 18th century people started to move to or visit Stamford Hill to escape the capital's pollution and enjoy the countryside, as at 109 ft above sea level the air was much cleaner than the centre of the city.

For some visitors it was not such a healthy place, as a gallows stood on Gibbet Field on the hill at the crossroads, perhaps as a warning to highwaymen, thieves and other ne'er do wells to stay away.

In 1738 a turnpike was sited on the London to Cambridge road on the hill to extract tolls from travellers, but the Rocques 1745 map shows little habitation at this time around the crossroads.

Hackney in the 18th century was noted for its attraction to other religions and many non-conformists, including Quakers and Jews, forbidden to practice their faiths in the City, found more tolerance just a few miles north. Religious freedom was becoming more acceptable after several Acts of Parliament such as the Five Mile Act 1665 and the Act of Toleration 1689.

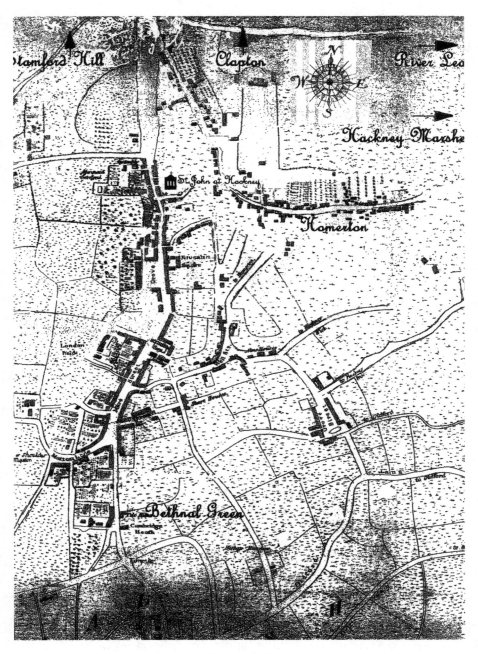

18th Century Hackney

18th Century Hackney

During the 18th century Hackney village was in a mostly bucolic, rural area northeast of the capital. In terms of distance not very far from disease ridden, polluted and congested central London but an entirely different way of life. The centre of Hackney village centred around the old parish church of St. John at Hackney and consisted of not much more than the properties fronting on to Church St. and little else beyond. Other separate outlying communities were springing up such as Homerton, Clapton, Stoke Newington, Stamford Hill and Kingsland before joining later to form the area known as Hackney today.

It was known as a place for a good day out, offering fishing, pleasure grounds, taverns and sporting events in a pleasant countryside environment. It was essentially a farming and agricultural area with market gardens, watercress beds fed from the Hackney Brook and supplying London with fruit and vegetables. Many nurseries, such as the world famous Loddiges, were set up in Hackney and also a number of brickfields were in the area.

There was abundant Lammas or common land for villagers to graze their livestock from Lammas day in August to Lady Day in March on Hackney Downs, London Fields Well street Common and especially on Hackney Marshes. This entitlement is relevant today as residents on the far side of the Marshes are fighting to stop their Lammas land being absorbed by the 2012 Olympics development.

Increasingly, many retired people or families wishing to move from the inner city built fine houses and villas there, and the local population prospered from the extra employment from the building and servicing of these homes. Hackney also became known for good private schools for the more well-to-do. William Maitland's 'History of London' [1756] describes "the village of Hackney being anciently celebrated for the numerous seats of the nobility and gentry occasioned a mighty resort thither of persons of all conditions from the City of London." The diarists Pepys and Evelyn in the 17th century reported they found Hackney an agreeable place to visit. Though this sounds like an idyllic place, the 18th century parish of St John had its problems.

One of the magistrates of Hackney Petty Sessions, Henry Norris [1676-1762], left a record of cases brought before him during the period 1730-1753 now in book form called 'Justice in 18th Century

Hackney' by the London Record Society edited by Ruth Paley [1991]. A minor case would have to brought by a complainant to the court and the magistrates would have to decide if a cause of action was needed. Very often mediation would solve the problem. An unpaid parish constable would be appointed every year, not a very desirable duty but the unlucky person would have to serve unless he could find or pay a substitute. If assistance was required he would put up a 'hue and cry' and parishioners were obliged to come to his aid under forfeit or punishment, as was the constable if he was derelict in his duty. Apart from serious crimes most incidents were dealt with locally with four main types of punishments. In the 18th century there were 200 crimes punishable by death, although most were commuted. Second would be banishment i.e sent to the colonies maybe never to return. The third type was physical, such as branding, whipping or the stocks to be pelted with whatever came to hand. The fourth and most frequent one was a fine.

Up to two thirds of the cases would be for assault of one kind or another and frequently for wife beating. Other cases may be for petty theft, such as burglary, stealing laundry or tools, and taverns prosecuted for serving drinks on a Sunday, which could result in losing their licence. The right to settlement, enabling an outsider to stay in the parish and claim relief, and also adjudging whether a relative had buried their recently deceased in wool would also come before the magistrates, both of which I will go into later.

My Gt. Grandfather {x5} Jonathan Adams appears once in the Petty Sessions records, in 1731, and was fined one shilling and sixpence for not maintaining the highway, presumably outside his property in Clopton {now Clapton} situated between Stamford Hill and Hackney Parish church.

The Petty Sessions book

> *366. The following persons were Summoned to appear before the said Justices this day to Shew cause why they have neglected to Perform their Statute on the Highwayes belonging to the **Parish of St John at Hackney** for the year 1731 and also why they have refused or neglected to pay Mr. Robert Aldwicncle and Mr Edward Nutt the Present Surveyrs for the defaults vizt –*

*Clopon: Henry Page Excused; *[blank] Bergaine to pay 9s.;
Thompson not sumoned; *John Windum to pay 4s, 6d.;
John Cawne paid 4. 6d,; *Margt. Gelding to pay 6s,; Wm
Hewson to be Excused on Condition he opens the Drains
in Clopton; Samuel Stower gone away; Wm. Stretton Junr
Excused; *Wido, Piller to pay 4s. 6.; *Willuam Darville
to pay 3s.; Mattw, Willson paid [apparently altered from
to pay] 4s.6.; *Wm. Boatman to pay 4. 6d.; Thos Sowden
paid 3s.; *John Wilmer to pay 1s 6d.; *John Hilliard to pay
3s.; Wm. Harris Excused; Christop Place; *Joseph Bourne
to pay s 6d.; *Wm. Knight to pay 4s 6d.; Philp Osborne
wll pay; Jane Wright not summoned; Isaac Portwny pd
1s. 6d.; *Jonath Adams to pay 1s. 6d.; Frans. Wheeler not
summoned; Edmund Matthew pd 6s.; Edward Cressell gone
away, Thos. Nicholls to wore 3 days, ; Joseph Cooper paid
4s. 6,; *Wido. Smith to pay 1s. 6d.; Thomas Archer paid
4s. 6d.; *Richd. Hawkins to pay 1s. 6d.*

Jonathan is shown as paying Land Tax in Clapton up until his death
in 1748. This was continued by his widow Rachel until 1767 for
the same property when a new name replaces her. Rachel Adams
died in 1770.

The population of Hackney at this time was quite small with barely
a thousand people paying tax of which one hundred and fifty were
in the Clapton area.

Even into the 19th century Hackney became the area of choice to live,
still being a desirable location especially with the increasing easier
access to the city with better roads and the coming of the railway in
the 19th century. Benjamin Clarke's "Glimpses of Ancient Hackney"
a hundred years after William Maitland's observations, describes
many of these fine people such as nobility, Members of Parliament,
churchmen, artists, businessmen and the more well to do with the
fine houses they built, and it seems until urban sprawl took over
Hackney in the 20th century it remained a desirable area.

Burials in wool

The following lists (356-60) of the names of dates (relating to burials in woollen) are collected from various places in the original manuscript.

Saturday 5 June 1736 E Blevin – Enoch Wratten & John Harrill.

Monday 21 June 1736 – D° – Rob: Revill Jn° Stillingfleet Jn° Woodfield.

Monday 28 June 1736 D° – Sa: Townsend & Jane Adams.

Saturday 3 July 1736 D° – El: Mayhew.

Tuesday 6 July 1736 Sa: Dobbs pr Tho: Marvell.

Saturday 10 July 1736 E Blevin pr Tho: Vandeclus Wm Bucknell Jno Wallis Jam: Coppin. Anne Fisher pr W^m. Harwood.

The demise of a loved one would have to be brought to the notice of the magistrates and an affidavit produced to them within 8 days stating a burial in wool. On the death of the infant Jane Adams, daughter of Jonathan and Rachell, in 1736 the proof is noted in the justicing notebook that she had been buried in wool as demanded in the 'Act for Burial in Wool' {1678} in force at this time This was brought in to protect the woollen trade and encourage the use of wool, an important industry in the 18th century, often smuggled abroad in exchange for tobacco, wine and spirits avoiding duty. The Act stated 'no corpse or any person {except those who die of the plague} shall be buried in any shirt, shift, sheet or shroud of anything whatsoever made or mingled with flax, hemp, hair, gold or silver or in any stuff or thing other than what is made of sheep's wool only'. This included the lining of coffins.

This meant if shrouds etc. were not made of wool a forfeiture or fine would be levied of £5 for using other materials. A considerable sum in the 17/18th century, probably equivalent today to several hundred pounds. Some of the wealthier mourners looked on it as another form of tax and so were willing to pay the fine for the sake of burying their loved one in, linen, satin, silk or some other type of shroud. If an informer made it known of such an unofficial burial to the authorities he would receive half of the fine and the rest go into parish funds. In some instances some families choosing the more expensive burial would inform on themselves, thus receiving the informers fee and reducing the cost by half. The Act was repealed by 1814 but by then was no longer effective.

With the advances in medical surgery during this period, a macabre trade in bodysnatching thrived to supply institutions with corpses for experimentation, and much despised and feared by the majority of the population. However, the practice itself was not illegal as the body now belonged to the earth but the shroud would have to be left or be classed as theft.

Settlement rights

The Settlement Act of 1662 along with the Removal Act are more properly known as the Poor Relief Acts, which endeavoured to better the lives of the poor people of their home parish and of the Kingdom generally by preserving their rights in hard times. Local magistrates would rule on eligibility. Before this act, travellers could go between different parishes and temporarily settle, use up any spare land and woods and perhaps burn and destroy property and moving on once the area was depleted. The Act sought to make each parish responsible for its parishioners born there or had been settled for some time.

Unless a newcomer had a premise paying a yearly rent of £10 or if they became a burden they could be removed to the parish where they were last legally settled. A person employed in the parish for over a year would be able to claim parish relief the same as a resident born there. In reality, employers were encouraged by the parish officers to let employees go before the year was up, sometimes after 364 days, and take on new workers thus removing their rights from perhaps being a future charge on the parish. A wife from outside the area would take on the husband's settlement rights.

On requesting parish relief when falling on hard times, if there was a dispute about the claimant's settlement rights the case would be examined by the magistrates before any assistance would be given. Once settled this would usually be in the form of cash or sometimes food, although barely enough to get by. A fate to befall John and Jonathan Adams and their family early in their lives.

From 1772, orphans, the poor but physically able and not too old parishioners were put to menial work in the local workhouse, a place best avoided, dreaded by many. Anyone refusing this was put out of the parish books and relief withdrawn.

Remains of Old St. John at Hackney Church
St. Augustine's Tower

The principal centre of activity in Hackney, has always been and remains today around the first parish church of St. John, originally called St. Augustine's, now in Mare Street from 1868 but was formerly known as Church Street. Mare is said to have derived not from an equine connection but from the old English word "meare" meaning a boundary, probably at its southern end where it adjoins Bethnal Green. The church was to figure in the lives of my ancestors for at least 70 years for carrying out baptisms, marriages and burials.

The parish covered a wide area from its centre as far as the borders of Tottenham, Stoke Newington and Bethnal Green with its easternmost side the River Lea which was also to play an important role for my family. The church, a Kentish ragstone structure, named St. Augustine's from at least the 14th century up to the 17th century, and it is believed there has been a place of worship on the site since 1250AD. In 1596 four bells were added to the tower, increased to six from 1678 and eight from 1743, along with a new clock replacing the original one from 1628.

It was decided in the late 18th century, to demolish and replace the existing ancient church with a new one as it was deemed to be too small for the expanding congregation, and so perhaps as a result would lose many of their flock to the various non-conformist churches now in Hackney.

Questions were asked at the time why it had to be destroyed as even after perhaps 500 years it was still in good condition, a mistake not made by neighbouring St. Mary's, Stoke Newington, when building their new church, as it still survives to this day. Some of the materials from the demolished St. John's went to build the bridge over Hackney Brook, a short distance away, necessary as it could be difficult and sometimes impossible to ford when in flood. The old church is in a slightly elevated position from the brook on the road to Clapton, always known to locals as the 'narroway', and so is unlikely to have been flooded often.

However, the new St. John's church, designed by James Spiller in the form of a large Greek cross, was built and completed and consecrated in 1797 and was designed to accommodate 3,000 people. Fortunately the new steeple, it was decided, was not strong enough to house the bells and so the bell tower of the old church was saved where it still stands to this day in Mare St. as a fine ancient monument. It was to be over fifty years before the church bells rang out in the new St.

John at Hackney tower once it was strengthened. The old belltower was latterly used as a sexton's tool house and a mortuary, but has been closed to the public for some time. I believe, and hope, there are plans to open up the old tower again as part of the refurbishment of the churchyard.

Allhallows Church Tottenham 1726

Jonathan Adams and Rachell Williams was Married by Banns on Sunday the 17 Day of July Anno Dom. 17__

St. John at Hackney Baptisms

Elizabeth of Jonathan Adams by Rachel his wife was Bapt. on the 7 day of April 1729

John of Jonathan Adams by Rachel his wife was Bapt. on the 30th day of May. 1731

a Rachel of Jonathan Adams by Rachel was Bapt. on the 15th day of Decemb. 1733

Jane of Jonathan Adams by Rachael was Bapt. on the 6th day of June 1736

St. John at Hackney Burials

Jane Adams (Inft) was Buried on the 22d day of June 17__

Jonathan Adams (collarmaker) was Buried — — — — — — Mar 20 17__

Family Tree Roots

This then was the parish of Hackney that John and Jonathan Adams were born into and also where the family lived for at least 70 years. After residing in different places in the East End of London over the next 150 years, their descendants returned to Hackney by the middle of the 20th century and it was where I was brought up, although born in Bethnal Green.

Having been put on the trail that the brothers were from Stamford Hill I set about tracing back as far as I could with any certainty, but as stated before, you may find the correct names but not accompanied by any backup information as to the right person or family. The choice of names was much more limited in the 18th century and usually passed father to son and mother to daughter for the first child of each sex, and after that perhaps taking grandparents names. This can be useful in some cases but you can't always be sure you are looking at the same family. I was fortunate in that some of the occupations were passed on and Christian names were ones that were not overused and continued through the following generations. Cross referencing parish births, marriages and burials with vestry and land tax records and some lateral thinking can help to justify some speculation.

My earliest ancestors I can be absolutely sure of are the grandparents of John and Jonathan Adams and their sisters Rachel and Dinah Jemima. The grandparents were another Jonathan Adams and his wife Rachell (née Williams) and I have found a record of their marriage in 1726 at Allhallows in Tottenham the next village north from Stamford Hill. In those days it would have been a short stroll across open fields between the two or a ride up the River Lea which will feature later.

I've not been able to confirm the births of these two but presumably they were born around the early years of the 18th century where I have found several Jonathan Adams' from north into Hertfordshire and south into central London, but nothing to prove it is the right one. I suspect Jonathan was from Hackney Parish and he married Rachell in her local church in Tottenham because before long they had children all baptised in St. John at Hackney. Also a man would not want to lose his settlement rights, as stated previously, and as his wife, Rachell would take on the same rights in her husband's home parish, as would any children born there.

John Adams was their first son born in 1731 and was to become my Gt. Grandfather [x5] and the father of Jonathan and his namesake John Adams the 'Bounty mutineer.' Other siblings were Elizabeth [1729], Rachel [1733], and Jane [1736] who died in infancy and who was the subject of the affidavit needed to confirm a burial in wool as also mentioned previously.

I believe soon after the marriage they were living in Clopton (now Clapton, old English for the farm on the hill), midway between Stamford Hill and the parish church along the ridge above the River Lea, around what is now Springfield Park. The reason for this assumption is the aforementioned appearance before magistrates when fined one shilling and sixpence for not maintaining the highway at Clopton.

Nothing more is known at the moment of the parents, except a burial recorded in 1747 at St. John at Hackney for a Jonathan Adams and an occupation given as 'collarmaker'.

At first I was not absolutely sure if this was the same Jonathan Adams although the population of Hackney was quite small at that time. The land tax records for Clapton seem to confirm it as a Jonathan Adams was no longer a tax payer by 1749. Soon after Jonathan's recorded death, payments were continued by a Rach[a]el Adams the same name as our Jonathan's wife. This linking of the two Christian names with the Adams surname must surely prove Rachael had been the deceased Jonathan Adams' wife and the grandmother of John and Jonathan Adams. She was to continue paying the land tax until 1767 by which time she must have been quite an elderly lady.

I wondered what Jonathan's occupation as a collar maker entailed in a rural area and then realised in those pre-mechanisation days collars would be worn by animals for towing ploughs, carts, barges etc. Unfortunately the land tax records do not give any indication of trades carried out on their property, but perhaps it was also the site of a workshop as well as a residence.

The proximity of the River Lea may have been a factor for the family to live in the Clapton/Stamford Hill area. This was the era of extensive movement of goods by barge and the River Lea was a faster highway for moving large loads to London and back from the River Thames rather than by road, due to their poor state unless they formed part of a toll road. I am of an age that remembers the canal barge trade of the 1950's in London and the huge leather collars the shire horses wore to pull the barges. Bargeman was to be the trade taken up by his son, John and so perhaps his father was able to fix up a job for him if he was making and repairing collars for horses. John would have been sixteen at the time his father died and so would already have been at work a number of years, and as his son John the mutineer made known in his brief account of his early life, his father worked for a coal merchant and died when he drowned in the River Thames surely as a River Lea bargeman. Barges would have been loaded with coal from Thameside docks such as Wapping or Ratcliffe, and transported to wharves along the River Lea.

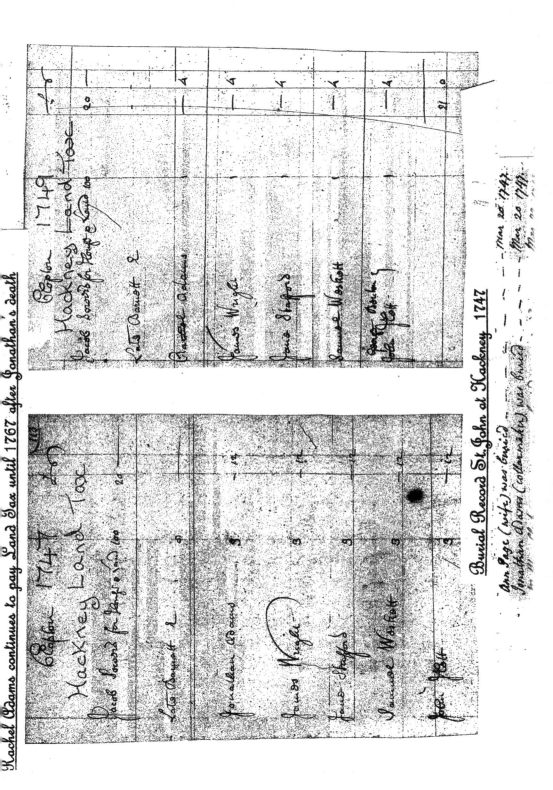

Rachel Adams continues to pay Land Tax until 1767 after Jonathan's death

Caplon 1747
Hackney Land Tax

Caplon 1749
Hackney Land Tax

Burial Record St. John at Hackney 1747

Ann Page (wife) was buried - - - Mar 22d 1747.
Jonathan Adams (collarmaker) was buried - - Mar 20 1749.

John Adams (1731-1783)

After the death of his father Jonathan in 1747, his only son would have become head of the family aged only sixteen, and with the early death of Jane, two surviving sisters and his mother to support. At such times as this, if no other help was available, the parish would supply basic assistance as long as Settlement Rights were in order. I've found no record of payments from Hackney Parish overseers at this time so perhaps the family were self sufficient and able to support themselves in other ways.

John Adams must have been married by 1754 as his first child Rachel, named after her grandmother, was born. After considerable searching of local and adjacent churches I've still not been able to come up with a marriage for John to Dinah. His job as bargeman on the River Lea would have him covering considerable distances to and from London and maybe north into Hertfordshire or east into Essex on the far side of the river and I believe that she may have come from outside the parish of St. John at Hackney or nearby villages.

After daughter Rachel was born the next child was Dinah Jemima born in 1757. Their first surviving son was John, the infamous mutineer born 1767 and followed by Jonathan my Gt Grandfather {x4} in 1774. There is a death registered in 1757 of a Dinah Jemima Adams seven months after the birth of their sister, and as the Christian names are unusual I presume it is the second daughter of John and Dinah. However, as many children died at a young age at these times the names were sometimes re-used. In his attempt to write his early life around 1800, John Adams mentioned he was one of four children when they became orphans so perhaps the Dinah Jemima that died was another branch of the family and a namesake for his sister. John Adams, a widower soon after the birth of Jonathan, was to die in tragic circumstances in 1783, nine years after his wife Dinah and these events may have had an effect on what was to follow later.

St. John at Hackney Baptisms

Rachel D. of John & Dinah Adams bap. — Dec. 4 1754.

Dinah Beatrice D. of John & Elizabeth Adams bap. — Feb 2 1757

John S. of John & Dinah Adams — Bap. 4 Dec. 1767

Jonathan S. of John & Dinah Adams — Bap. 13. Apr. 1774.

Death of Dinah Adams Mother

Dinah Adams   Buried 6. Nov. 1774.

Doctor Livingstone presumed

Although I have no proof of her later life, according to the Bounty Genealogies by P.J. Lareau, eldest daughter Rachel Adams, sister of John and Jonathan, has some interesting descendants. It seems she married a James Smith, nurseryman, of Dukinfield near Manchester although it states in the Gentlemen's Magazine it was Derby.

The genealogy goes on to say they had a daughter Mary who married Robert Moffat a well known missionary in the early 19th century. The Moffat's daughter also Mary, married David Livingstone, missionary and explorer and they both spent many years in Africa.

Tim Jeal's biography states Mary Livingstone was no great beauty and in later life became very fat and an alcoholic, but Livingstone needed a wife and the choices in Africa were very limited. Mary was brought up in Africa and unlike many women was able to stand the rigours of life in the harsh environment and so suited Livingstone's selfish needs. Completely focused on his missions, his wife and children were often left to fend for themselves, short of food and decent clothing.

In 1852 he sent Mary and four children under seven back to Britain with little money, expecting the London Missionary Society to provide for them. In fact what was to follow was four and a half years of poverty and a nomadic existence, having to accept charity, moving between various friends and family. Apart from staying with David's parents in Scotland who Mary found too severe, other places they stayed were Kendal, Epsom, Manchester and Hackney. Although this was quite a long time after the Adams's had left Hackney was it possible there was still some connections in the parish where her grandmother was born? Mary expected David after two years to return but it was to be four and a half before she saw him. They returned to Africa but after a hard life with a harsh husband and increasingly turning to drink Mary caught malaria and died of the fever in 1862.

Another interesting item in Tim Jeal's biography is a mention of a cockney labourer described as an agriculturist name of Adams, on the Universities Mission expedition, but no further details. The mentions of Hackney, Manchester and a cockney named Adams the agriculturist [nurseryman?] connections are intriguing but as yet not conclusive. The theory of John and Jonathan's sister Rachel marrying a nurseryman may be feasible as Hackney had many nurseries and market gardens in the 18th century, including the world famous Loddiges which was one of many in the area. A German family, the Loddiges set up in business in Hackney in the mid 18th century in the area now known as Loddiges/Frampton Park Roads, and collected plants worldwide that would not normally thrive in England's climate. The plants were developed in a hothouse situation by a steam central heating system and were able to produce palms, and orchids and at more temperate temperatures ferns and camellias. By 1860 the business closed and all that is left is the name of the road where it stood among 15 acres.

So it is quite possible that John Smith may have worked in, or ran a nursery locally and they may have met in a place common to everybody, such as the parish church. If true, it would make John and Jonathan Adams Great Uncles to the wife of the famous Dr. David Livingstone and may warrant further investigation at a later date.

Dinah Adams {?-1774}

With the arrival of her fourth known surviving child, my Gt. Grandfather {x4} Jonathan in 1774, his mother Dinah having had her first child Rachel twenty years before was probably at an advanced age to have another baby. This seems to be the start of the family's misfortunes and may have been the catalyst for the fate of her children later in life. Within six months of the birth of Jonathan, Dinah is mentioned in the burial register of St. John at Hackney, but no details as to cause of death. John would have been seven years old and his brother still a baby and daughter Rachel was probably married by this time, as John Adams stated from Pitcairn that one was married and out of all harms way. He mentions three children still left so the Dinah Jemima that died perhaps was not a sister or it was not unknown for a subsequent child to take the same names of a deceased sibling. Their father must have struggled to cope, as within a few weeks he was forced to go to the parish for assistance. This was granted at the rate of 2 shillings a week and continued for some time according to parish records and then withdrawn perhaps as circumstances improved.

This proves the importance of Settlement Rights, as explained previously, to enable a parishioner to call on the parish in times of strife.

Fortunately the Adams family were firmly established in the St. John at Hackney area for at least fifty years. Without these rights the home parish would be decided by the magistrates and the family moved on to the next parish where they would probably get the same treatment until the agreed Settlement parish was reached.

Up to 1780 the family must have coped somehow as they do not appear to have applied for relief for a few years. However, by December of that year I have an entry in Hackney Workhouse records for Jonathan Adams, now aged six. John Adams in his brief life history, stated they were in the workhouse but I've found no entry for John himself so I think at the age of 13 his stay may have been brief and could have been the start of his sea-going career. There is also a child, Dinah Adams, three years older than Jonathan in the workhouse, but no traceable connection as yet as she is fourteen years younger than his sister Dinah Jemima but possibly a relative of some description.

Jonathan's entries in the workhouse continue for three more years and then he disappears after that from the records perhaps rescued by his brother from that harsh institution as their father was no longer around. The next mention of the two brothers is on the deck of the Bounty at Deptford saying their farewells in 1787.

Hackney Workhouse

The local parish workhouse for St. John at Hackney came into being in 1732 when a house was rented and repaired for use by the parish. By 1741 it had moved to a house rented on the south side of Homerton High St opposite the Adam and Eve pub and what is now the site of Hackney Hospital. According to the rules and orders of the workhouse in the late 18th century it was run as a strict regime, but supplied everything for basic survival. The children of the workhouse, many of them orphans, were kept until they were twelve or thirteen and then apprenticed out to a master usually for a fee to learn a trade or to go into service, thus relieving the orphanage of feeding and clothing them for longer than necessary. The following examples are extracts from the list of twenty-one rules from a document at Hackney Archives as they were in 1764. Originally run by a master at 3 shillings per week, per inmate, it soon became clear it was not being run properly. Therefore it was taken back by the committee and they employed a new master on a salary of £30 pounds per year.

RULES AND ORDERS OF THE WORKHOUSE

<u>II</u> THAT PRAYERS BE SAID IN THIS HOUSE EVERY MORNING BY THE MISTRESS OR SOMEONE DEPUTED BY HER, BEFORE BREAKFAST;AND EVERY EVENING BEFORE SUPPER;AND THAT GRACE BE SAID BEFORE AND THANKS RETURNED AFTER EACH MEAL; AND THOSE THAT ARE ABLE,AND DO NOT ATTEND PRAYERS TO LOSE THEIR DINNER.

<u>III</u> ALL THAT ARE ABLE AND IN HEALTH TO GO EVERY SUNDAY TO CHURCH OR SOME OTHER PLACE OF RELIGIOUS WORSHIP, MORNING AND AFTERNOON; THAT THEY RETURN HOME AS SOON AS DIVINE SERVICE IS OVER; AND IF ANY BE FOUND LOITERING OR BEGGING BY THE WAY, TO LOSE THEIR NEXT MEAL. IF AT ANY TIME THEY GET DRUNK OR ARE GUILTY OF PROPHANE CURSING OR SWEARING, TO BE PUNISHED IN THE STOCKS AS THE LAW DIRECTS.

<u>IV</u> THAT NO PERSON BE PERMITTED TO GO OUT OF THE HOUSE WITHOUT LEAVE UNLESS UPON SOME GREAT EMERGENCY......... AND IF THEY DO NOT RETURN WITHIN THE TIME ALLOWED THEM THEN THE MISTRESS DO NOT PRESUME TO LET THEM INTO THE HOUSE AGAIN .....

<u>V</u> THAT NO DISTILLED LIQUORS BE BROUGHT INTO THE HOUSE WITHOUT LEAVE FROM THE COMMITTEE, NOR ANY STRONG BEER WITHOUT LEAVE FROM THE MISTRESS; AND WHOEVER SHALL DISTURB THE HOUSE BY BRAWLING, QUARRELLING, FIGHTING, OR ABUSIVE LANGUAGE SHALL LOSE ONE DAY'S MEAL AND FOR THE SECOND OFFENCE BE PUT IN THE DARK ROOM TWENTY FOUR HOURS.

<u>VI</u> THAT EVERY PERSON IN HEALTH SHALL BE KEPT TO SUCH LABOUR AS THEY CAN WELL DO, ACCORDING TO THEIR SEVERAL AGES AND ABILITIES; AND THAT IS TO SAY FROM LADY-DAY TO MICHAELMAS FROM SIX OF THE CLOCK IN THE MORNING TO SIX AT NIGHT; FROM MICHAELMAS TO LADY-DAY FROM SEVEN IN THE MORNING

TILL FIVE AT NIGHT [MEAL-TIME EXCEPTED]: AND IF ANY GROWN PERSON REFUSE TO WORK, TO BE KEPT ON BREAD AND WATER, OR EXPELLED THE HOUSE; THE CHILDREN TO BE CORRECTED BY THE MISTRESS.

VIII THAT A BELL BE RUNG EVERY MORNING, IN THE SUMMER FROM LADY-DAY TO MICHAELMAS BY FIVE AND FROM MICHAELMAS TO LADY-DAY BY SIX, FOR THE HEALTHFUL PEOPLE TO RISE TO WORK: AND TO GO TO BED IN THE SUMMER BY NINE. AND IN THE WINTER BY EIGHT; AND THAT THE MISTRESS SEE ALL THE CANDLES OUT AT THAT TIME.

X THAT ALL CHILDREN BE WASHED, COMBED AND CLEANED BY EIGHT IN THE MORNING AND SOME PROPER PERSONS TO TEACH THEM TO READ; AND THEY MAY BE TAUGHT TO LABOUR AND WORK AS THE COMMITTEE SHALL DIRECT, IN SUCH MANUFACTURES AS BE MOST USE-FUL AND BENEFICIAL FOR THE PUBLICK GOOD; AND NOT PERMITTED TO PLAY TILL THEY HAVE FINISHED THEIR TASKS.

XVII DAILY FOOD PER ADULT. 7OZS OF MEAT WHEN DRESSED WITHOUT BONES, 2OZS BUTTER, 4 OZS CHEESE, 1 LB BREAD, 3 PINTS BEER. CHILDREN AT DISCRETION OF MISTRESS.

XVIII THAT EVERY PERSON ENDEAVOUR TO PRESERVE A GOOD UNITY AND LOOK UPON THEMSELVES AS ON FAM-ILY AND TO PREVENT ANY DISPUTE WHICH MAY CREATE DIFFERENCES AMONGST THEMSELVES BY FORGING AND TELLING LIES.SUCH PERSONS SO OFFENDING [ON GOOD PROOF OF THE COMMITTEE] SHALL BE SET ON A STOOL IN THE MOST PUBLICK PLACE IN THE DINING ROOM WHILST THE FAMILY ARE AT DINNER AND A PAPER FIXED ON HIS OR HER BREAST WITH THESE WORDS WROTE" INFAMOUS LYAR" AND LIKEWISE TO LOSE THAT MEAL.

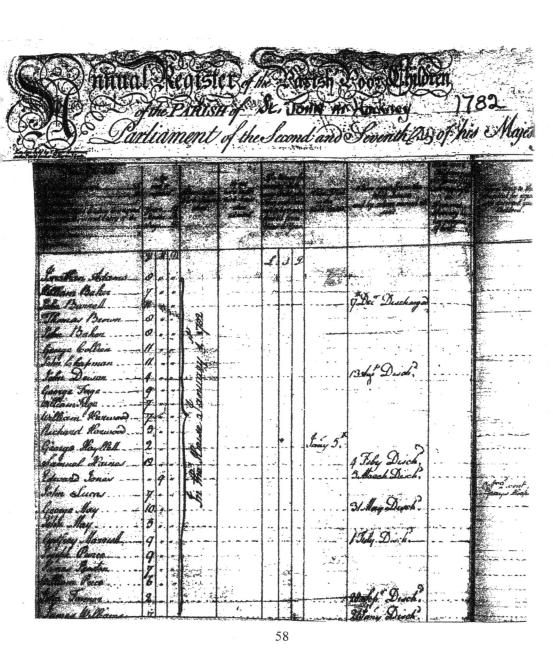

Register of St. John at Hackney Workhouse, January 1782

Daniel Bell, employer of John Adams

I think at this stage it is important to look at the life of John Adams, the father of John and Jonathan Adams, and perhaps see why their lives turned out the way they did, one a mutineer in hiding, yet the patriarch of a South Sea island, and the other to become an upright member of his community in London, The occupation of their father is again known from the brief account by John setting down on Pitcairn Island his early life in Hackney and that his father worked for a Daniel Bell, coal merchant. In trying to find out more about John's job by researching his employer, I found that the Bells were a renowned Quaker family and very important in the Tottenham and Hackney area.

Quakers are usually regarded as peace-loving, devout, respectable and hardworking members of the community, but this belies their radical beginnings. Formed around 1650, it was led by a shoemaker's apprentice from Leicestershire named George Fox. Religious upheaval, leading to disruption, ensued which sometimes meant prison for some protesting offenders when they wished to break away from the established Anglican church to be able to carry out their own form of worship.

Refusing to serve in the military or pay tithes, they were seen as dangerous subversives and a threat to society. The name Quakers is said to have derived from their trembling at visitations or from the word of the Lord. Anxious to discourage these non-conformists the government and the monarchy of Charles II, in the mid 17th century brought in Acts of Parliament to disrupt the dissenters' meetings.

The Conventicle Act of 1664 forbade religious assemblies of more than five people, unless in Anglican churches, causing ministers to leave their parishes and hold meetings in the open air.

This was followed by the Five Mile or Oxford Act of 1665, another act for restraining non-conformists and enforcing conformity. The Act forbade dissenting clergymen from living within five miles of a parish from which they had been banned unless they swore an oath never to resist the King or attempt to deny the government of church or state.

During the reign of William and Mary in 1689 the Act of Toleration was passed granting freedom of worship to dissenters apart from Unitarians and Catholics and the repeal of the Conventicle and

Five Mile Acts. In return they were to make a solemn declaration of loyalty instead of an oath of allegiance and to declare their belief in the doctrine of the Holy Trinity and inspiration from the Bible. Renamed the Society of Friends, they went on to succeed in the business world, always plainly dressed, modestly spoken and regarded to be straight and fair in their business transactions. Many names familiar today, at the forefront of commerce and industry, such as Barclays and Lloyds banks, Clarks shoes and Huntley and Palmers have their roots from the Quakers.

Looking for an alternative to encourage people away from alcohol, the manufacture of chocolate was taken up by some Quaker families, including Fry's, Cadbury's and Rowntree's, still major names today. George Fox, the founder died in 1691 so lived to see Quakerism, although not fully understood by many, accepted and flourishing.

Daniel Bell, John senior's employer, was a prominent Quaker businessman trading in coal by barge along the River Lea to and from the Thames. He had at least one wharf at Stamford Hill at the end of what is now Craven Park Road {formerly Bell's Lane on the Tottenham border). I think it is safe to assume that as John stated his father drowned in the Thames that he worked on one of the barges transporting coal. Not entirely true about the location of his death but more of that later.

The Bells were a prosperous and devoutly Quaker family originally from Cockermouth in Cumberland, coincidentally where Fletcher Christian's family were from.

The Quakers were a close-knit community very much involved in business and because of the religious tolerance towards the end of the 18th century in the area, as mentioned previously, they were able to set up their own meeting house in Tottenham. The Bells were related to the Hanbury family, later to become Allen, Hanbury pharmaceuticals. They lived in one of the finest houses in Tottenham no great distance from Daniel's wharf on the River Lea, Daniel was the father of Priscilla Bell {1751-1832}, later Wakefield, who was the writer of many educational books for children on science, travel and natural history and the founder of the first Frugality Bank. She turned to writing after the failure of her husband's business. She was also the aunt of Elizabeth Fry {1780-1845} the prison reformer, who is featured currently on the back of the £5 note.

Finally it is interesting to note that two men signed on for the Bounty voyage but deserted before she sailed, were named as Robert Barclay and William Bell. Both surnames are associated with London Quakerism, the latter perhaps a relation of John Adams senior's employer Daniel Bell, Both men were in their early twenties in 1789 when the Bounty sailed and possibly were connected in some way, but is pure speculation at the moment.

Trade on the River Lea

The late 18th century and the early part of the 19th century was the peak of movement of goods by the widespread network of canals and waterways until the arrival of the railways. Large loads could be moved much more quickly than on the poorly maintained road system.

The demand for coal in the outer reaches of London and beyond would have given Daniel Bell a ready market by transporting loads upriver from the banks of the River Thames through the Lea Valley to Essex, Middlesex and Hertfordshire. Perhaps a return load of wheat, malt or barley, abundant upstream, would be found for the empty barge returning to the Thames and central London. Bow, downstream from Hackney on the River Lea, was particularly noted for its bakeries supplying the City and would need corn and wheat and breweries the malt. Living in Stamford Hill or Clapton it would have been a short walk for John Adams to the coal wharves on the River Lea where the horse drawn or sailing barges would be moored.

The River Lea, sometimes called Lee, rises in Bedfordshire and is believed to have been navigable since Roman times. This gave them a route to Verulanium {St.Alban's} from Londinium {London} via the Thames at Blackwall. King Alfred was said to have pursued the Danes upriver in the 9th century A.D. For the last part of its journey south it also forms a boundary between Middlesex on the west side and Essex to the east. It has been a source of fresh water for hundreds of years, some eventually being channelled off to form the New River leading to Sadler's Wells in North London.

The Lea was known as a good river for fishing and Izaak Walton, author of 'The Compleat Angler' mentions fishing the upper reaches. Daniel Bell would have purchased his coal around the Wapping, Ratcliffe and Shadwell area wharves where there was a Bell Wharf Stairs and a Coal Stairs, on the north bank of the Thames. The coal would have arrived in collier boats from the northeast of England. These flat-bottomed boats, similar to the Bounty were suitable for carrying heavy cargoes and were built mainly in Whitby and Scarborough. They were able to sail out to sea and also in shallow waters, an average voyage, depending on tides and weather, took seven days. Captain James Cook, the famous explorer, learnt his trade on these boats as an apprentice and were later used for his South Seas explorations. For a time he lived in Shadwell and Mile End after marrying a Wapping publican's daughter. Once the collier boats arrived they would be unloaded, no easy task, as there would have been heavy congestion in the Thames with hundreds of boats waiting for a berth. It has been said a person would be able to walk from one side of the river to the other without getting their feet wet.

Collier boats anxious to turn around and get underway, unless pre-arrangements were made, could wait for weeks to be unloaded. Once unloaded into barges or lighters [so called because they lightened the ship after removing the cargo] the coal would begin its onward journey. For Daniel Bell's barges this would be via Limehouse and the New Cut to Bow and the River Lea. This route avoided the long way around the Isle of Dogs to Blackwall and the meandering Lea to the River Thames. There was a significant Quaker influence in

Ships unloading in the busy Pool of London. In the foreground is a coal barge being loaded, possibly for the River Lea trade. Part of the Rheinbeck Panorama. Courtesy of the Museum of London.

this dockland area with Friend's Meeting Houses nearby in Wapping and Ratcliffe. The Quaker community was very well thought of and were charitable to not just their own brethren but assisting many other families fallen on hard times, with food and medical aid. Daniel Bell must have known and dealt with many of these fellow Quakers, perhaps also in the coal trade.

The Death of John Adams

By the time of my Gt. Grandfather {x4} Jonathan's birth in 1774 the family of John Adams and his wife Dinah seemed to be no worse than many at the time. With at least 3 surviving children and living by all accounts in a desirable part of the country. Daniel Bell, as a Quaker, was presumably a good employer and a job working on his barges, although hard work, would have been preferable I think to that of the other main country occupation as an agricultural labourer. I believe things started to go wrong after Jonathan was born, when within 6 months his mother died. Whether this was due to complications after the birth, as she must have been coming to the end of her childbearing days, or was struck down by disease, such as the smallpox that affected John Adams will probably never be known. The burial register only states her name and date of her interment. Inquests or post-mortems would only be carried out for suspicious or unusual deaths. The affect on the family was felt within a short time, as John Adams approached the Parish Overseers and was granted assistance of 2 shillings [10 pence] per week 3 weeks later on 28th November 1774 and drew it consistently until 22 May the following year. In the years 1776 and 1777 he only drew money during the winter months of January and February and at the reduced rate of 1 shilling [5 pence] or 1 shilling and sixpence [7½ pence] per week.

This may have been because the River Lea may not have been navigable or it was not unknown for the River Thames to be frozen over thus preventing the movement of the barges even though the demand for coal would have been greater.

John Adams first request for parish relief and granted two shillings per week. 28/11/1774. Wife Rachell buried three weeks previously. John aged 7 and Jonathan 6 months.

By 1780 the pressure of looking after his family must have been too great and his sons John and Jonathan were put in the Hackney Workhouse just before Christmas, Although not orphans yet, I have found some original information which throws some light on his inability to cope and the manner of his death. This was an old document buried in the archives dated 1783 and I may have been the first person to open it since then. After studying it, due to its age I was not allowed to photocopy it, so paid for a laser scan. On a later visit it was deemed too fragile to handle and is now only viewable on microfilm. The document was about 18 inches square and was a printed form used for coroner's inquests with spaces to fill in with the deceased's details. This consisted of the place and cause of John Adams's death and was brought before an inquest jury to decide to the manner and circumstances of his demise.

Going back to John Adams' description of the death of his father in which he stated his father drowned in the Thames was true, insomuch as the nature of his death, but not the location. The document gives the place of drowning as the New Cut which was a purpose built canal sanctioned by the River Lee Act of 1766 and is now the oldest canal in London, It ran between the River Lea at Bromley-by-Bow and the River Thames at Limehouse. This route cut out the lower reaches of the Lea, difficult to navigate, thus creating a short cut avoiding the long way round the Isle of Dogs and the necessity to wait on the tides. The exit to the Thames is now infilled and a new canal built to Regent's Canal Dock. The journey would have been part of the route often taken by Daniel Bell's coal barges and well known to John Adams.

The location may have been an easy mistake to make as an exact spot is not known and may have been a short distance from the end of the New Cut at its entry into the Thames at Limehouse. What is known is that the inquest was called because it was not a simple drowning but a "suicide whilst lunatic'. This route is now being used to transport materials by barge to the 2012 Olympics site alongside the River Lea on Hackney Marshes.

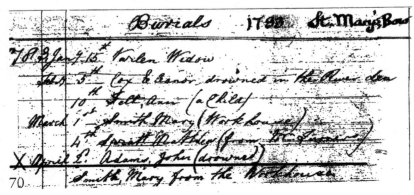

Church of St Mary's, Stratford at Bow ~
John Adams (1731-1783) burial place

St. Mary's Stratford, Bow is not to be confused with the "Bow Bells' of the Cockney origin story. The legend states that a true cockney should be born within the sound of Bow Bells, but this refers to the church in Cheapside in the City.

A temporary insanity or the reason for placing his children in the workhouse just over two years previously? The inquest was held in Bow, so named after the ancient bow shaped bridge which had taken the place of the Old Ford just upstream across the River Lea, above where the New Cut enters. No actual location is known for the inquest but it would often take place in a tavern and there were a number of those in the area on the main Aldgate to Essex road via Stratford.

The inquest document, like most legal documents, is long winded and repetitive but needed to be so to cover all aspects of a unnatural death, and is dated "the second day of April in the twenty third year of the reign of our sovereign Lord George the Third......" [1783]. The coroner was Thomas Phillips and a jury of 13 'good and lawful men of the said county' were duly chosen and sworn upon their oath to inquire how the said John Adams came to his death.

That 'the said John Adams not being of sound mind, memory and understanding but lunatic and distracted on the thirty first day of March in the year aforesaid, himself, into a cut of water called the New Cut situate in the Parish and County aforesaid, did cast and throw. By means whereof he the said John Adams was in the water of the said Cut then and there suffocated and drowned of which said suffocation and drowning he the said John Adams then and there died and so the jurors aforesaid upon their oaths aforesaid do say that the said John Adams not being of sound mind, memory and understanding but lunatic and distracted in manner by the means aforesaid did kill himself.'

IN WITNESS whereof, as well as the said coroner as the said John Dalby the Foreman of the said Jurors, on the behalf of himself and the rest of his said fellows, in their presence, have, to this inquisition, set their hands and seals, the day and the year first above written.

Thos Phillips   Coroner

Jonathan Adams' early life

The Register of Parish of Poor Children in Hackney Workhouse shows the last yearly entry after 3 years on 1st January 1783 for Jonathan Adams aged 9 years old, just three months before the death of his father.

However, the following year he does not appear on the register and as yet there is no trace of him leaving or his whereabouts until he is said to be on the deck of the Bounty at Deptford in 1787 saying farewell to his brother John and his re-appearance again in 1789 as an apprentice waterman. Could the death of their father kept them together until John decided at thirteen, Jonathan was capable of looking after himself which would probably have been true after his years in the workhouse? Having no immediate family left in Hackney, Jonathan may himself have gone to sea guided by his elder brother. Later years were to prove that he had the ability to make something of his life and so I think that was the case. Possibly the two brothers may already have spent time at sea prior to the Bounty voyage but is difficult to prove as records for ordinary seaman are not as traceable as for officers.

Alexander Smith

Whilst checking through the registers of St. John at Hackney I looked for clues for the name change of John Adams when signing on the Bounty. Smith is one of the commonest English surnames and even Alexander Smith was not an unusual name but someone about to use an alias would surely have to relate it to a person known to them to more easily remember.

St. John at Hackney Baptism July 1752

Charlotte Daughter of Mr James Graham by Sarah his wife was baptized July 14 1752
Alexander son of Michael & Mary Smith was baptized — — July 16 1752
Sarah Daught of John & Mary Burling was baptiz'd — — July 19 1752

I found a baptism in the register of St. John's in 1752 for an Alexander Smith making him two years older than John's sister Rachel who is said to have married a John Smith. Could Alexander have perhaps been a brother to John Smith and, that being fifteen years older than John Adams someone he looked up to and as a brother-in-law easier to bring to mind? Also around the time the Bounty sailed there is an Alexander Smith living in St. George in the East near to the docks of Wapping and Shadwell, perhaps also another acquaintance.

The choice of name change is one of the enduring mysteries of the Bounty story and will probably never be resolved. However, during my searches I have perhaps found a reason for the change of identity. Two events happened in the year 1787 within a short space of time in the Adams' home parish of St. John at Hackney just months prior to the sailing of the Bounty, The first is a marriage between a John Adams and Sarah Chappell on the 9th June. The signatures are both legible and the one for John Adams looks remarkably like later examples from Pitcairn Island.

*Signatures thought to have been used by John Adams
during his lifetime*

The next event is a baptism on 21st September, three months later, for Sarah daughter of John and Hannah Adams. Parish after the entry meaning probably that the mother had sought assistance, perhaps sent to the workhouse, due to an absentee father. By this time John Adams [as Alexander Smith] would have been preparing to sail on the Bounty.

Could it be he absconded and left behind the responsibility of a wife and child and the change of name was an intention not to return?

Of course the mother's name is given as Hannah and the daughter as Sarah but perhaps in a state of grief or anxiety the names could have been transposed, and it was also not unknown for names to have been transcribed wrongly. Another interesting fact is that John Adams on Pitcairn Island named two of his daughters after his sisters Rachel and Dinah and the third one Hannah.

Reward

Another piece of the Alexander Smith puzzle comes from an article I have never seen mentioned anywhere else that I unearthed in the Mitchell Library in Sydney. It is handwritten but with no provenance as to its origins and is as follows:

The Reward of a Bounty Mutineer

The mutiny on board HMS Bounty in 1789, the remarkable career of the survivors on the Pitcairn Island and the subsequent exodus of those people to Norfolk Island are matters of history, but facts which have recently come to light revive interest in the event [says the New Zealand Herald].

John Adams while serving on a man-of-war under his real name, Alexander Smith, saved the life of a midshipman on board by bravely jumping after him when he went overboard. The young man on returning home related his narrow escape, and his relatives, desirous of acknowledging the brave conduct of Smith, who could not then be found, placed £100 to his credit in the bank, the interest to accumulate until the reward was claimed. Many Smiths have claimed the reward but were unable to establish their claims or identify themselves with the man-of-war of the incident.

John Adams, the Bounty mutineer or Alexander Smith as he actually was has left three grandchildren in Norfolk Island. John the eldest grandson, who is now over 60 years of age, being informed of the circumstances, proceeded recently to Sydney to establish the claim of the family.

It is said that he thoroughly succeeded in identifying his grandfather with the plucky seaman who rescued this officer from a watery grave, and after placing the affair in the hands of a respectable firm of solicitors in Sydney, has now returned to Norfolk Island. Will it be believed that the investment of £100, some time prior to 1789, has now accumulated by interest and compound interest to the vast sum of £96,000? And yet this is the sum said to be now available for subdivision amongst the descendants of John Adams, the leader in the Bounty mutiny. The facts as connected with the mutiny of the Bounty are so much matters of history that is it hardly necessary to refer to them. When Pitcairn Island was visited by the British frigates, Briton and Tagus in 1814, there was a population of 48 but only two of the original mutineers were survivors, and of these Alexander Smith who had assumed the name of John Adams was one.

[n.b. Not true. The last survivor apart from John Adams was George Young, who died from lung disease in 1800.]

He was at the head of the colony, and was looked up to with the greatest reverence, and not undeservedly, as his character had undergone a thorough change, and he had not only led a moral and religious life but succeeded in imbuing his little community with similar habits. He died in 1829 at the age of 63.

[Extract from Daily Telegraph, 12ᵗʰ December 1888]

At a time when very few sailors could swim, if true, this would seem to have been a brave act. If this is the same John Adams, his ability to swim may have been due to him assisting his father on the barges and the proximity of the River Lea during his childhood. A dangerous place to fall into for a non-swimmer, proven by the number of graves in riverside churches attributed to drowning, and was finally to claim the life of his father although from suicide. I've been in touch with Auckland City Libraries that hold archived copies of the New Zealand Herald but cannot verify this story at the moment.

21st Century Hackney

The Hackney left behind by the two brothers in the 18th century is vastly different today from the rural, bucolic and desirable area to live in during their early lives.

Present day Hackney has even changed, not for the better, since my early life when as part of a slum clearance in Columbia Road, Bethnal Green, home of the famous Sunday flower market, we were moved to Hackney in the 1950s. Our new location in South Hackney on the borders of Victoria Park. Well St Common and Hackney Marshes, in retrospect, was a better area than some. Once on the fringes of London by the 20th century it had become part of the urban sprawl, eventually incorporated into Greater London and changed from an agricultural society to inner city deprivation. Never very affluent in the 20 years I lived there but at the time it seemed no worse than other East End boroughs post WWII but has recently been labelled the worst borough in England. There are probably many reasons for this that I am not qualified to comment on but poor housing, overcrowding and lack of investment may be contributing factors, although this may change with the coming of the 2012 Olympics to the area.

Many of the fine, large buildings are still standing, as a reminder of more affluent times, and in some areas attempts are being made to gentrify streets. For some prospective buyers the proximity of the City of London, no more than a few miles away, is an incentive to reduce commuting time. However, these large houses are also ideal now for multi-occupancy and as it always has done for many years attracts immigrants from all over the world creating a cosmopolitan look to some areas.

In 1801, Hackney was one of the few areas to have a census taken and the population was given as 12,730. The 2001 census states that the known population of the borough was 202,000 with 44% described as White British although 66% born in the United Kingdom. It is predominately a Christian area at 47% with a mixture of many other religions. Police sources in Ridley Road market in Kingsland Road say that they had over 30 different language translators on their books, which shows the cultural diversity of that part of Hackney.

Above: 18ᵗʰ century view of Hackney Brook and Church Street, now Mare Street, by Samuel Prout (Hackney Archives)
Below: present day view looking north to St Augustine's Tower

Many notable people have lived or were born in Hackney, amongst them sportsmen, writers, politicians and stars of the media and music industry. Lenin, Samuel Coultard, Edith Cavell and Joseph Priestley are known to have stayed in Hackney. Daniel Defoe had a house in Stoke Newington and Edgar Allan Poe attended school in the area.

Sir Francis Beaufort, appointed in 1829 Head of the Hydrographic Office of the British Admiralty and inventor of the Beaufort scale of wind measurement that bears his name [e.g. Force 8; 34-40 nautical miles per hour], is buried in Hackney churchyard. He is also credited with bringing together Captain Fitzroy of the Beagle, and Charles Darwin for their epic five year exploration and charting of South America, particularly the Galapagos Islands, by way of Tierra del Fuego and the notorious Cape Horn, which had beaten back Bligh over forty years before. The voyage was to form the basis for Darwin's controversial Origin of Species.

A tenuous connection to the Bounty is that Beaufort's rival for the job was Peter Heywood [now a Captain] the former young midshipman falsely condemned by Bligh but eventually pardoned leaving Bligh in a poor light. However, Heywood .the last surviving officer of the Bounty was dead within two years of applying for the post. The last surviving crew member of the Bounty was William Purcell, carpenter dying in 1834.

The Loddiges family, internationally known from the 18th century for the nursery and market garden established by Conrad Loddiges, also have a tomb in Hackney churchyard.

John Adams, {no relation as far as I know), the 2nd President of the United States, and previously ambassador to the Court of St. James's is said to have attended the Gravel Pit Chapel. Major John Andre hanged by Washington as a spy and John Howard penal reformer are also from Hackney.

Dr Robert Knox, anatomist, was infamous for purchasing cadavers from body snatchers Burke and Hare in Edinburgh, shunned from practising in Scotland, set up in Hackney presumably where he was less well known. Other residents in the public eye have been Dr Barnado, whose orphanages still bear his name, and Catherine and William Booth founders of the Salvation Army.

In the 20th century pop stars Marc Bolan and Helen Shapiro, entertainer Anthony Newley, Amstrad entrepreneur Alan Sugar, actor Ray Winstone, comedian Mike Reid, prankster Jeremy Beadle, footballers

Ron 'Chopper' Harris and Rodney Marsh and playwright Harold Pinter are all from Hackney. Henry Allingham, born in Clapton in 1896, was in 2009 the oldest person ever in Britain and one of the few survivors of the First World War. A character named 'Blind Fred' Peters, [1871-1933]. blind from birth, was well known for selling matches in Hackney churchyard for over 40 years. A memorial plaque in the graveyard commemorates his life with the inscription:- 'Hereby was seen for many years. Blind Fred, a sunny soul'.

The braille message below states:- 'One thing I know, that whereas I was blind now I see' [John 9.25].

Jack Cohen, founder of Tesco, after WW1 set up in business with a stall in Well St. Market and insisted on having a store there when his empire expanded. The ultimate irony now seems to be is that what used to be a thriving market, and one I used frequently, mostly for the pie and mash and the ice cream shops, is now in danger of disappearing with a lack of stalls, according to local people because of the updated Tesco Metro store, Others may say the market is just a victim of the way we choose to do our shopping today.

St.Augustine's bell tower from the original St. John at Hackney still dominates Mare St., [formerly Church St], saved when the new church was built, a short walk across the graveyard, over 200 years ago and is amongst over 1300 listed buildings in the borough. Sutton Manor is a fine Tudor manor house built in 1535, named after Thomas Sutton founder of Charterhouse school and hospital, although it is said he only lived nearby and not in the house. It has survived many changes of use and dereliction but is now back to its former glory under the National Trust.

Unfortunately, today where open country used to be in the late 18th century and the Adams family walked to the parish church for at least a period of 60 years, over fields and paths from Clapton and Stamford Hill, has now become a dangerous place. Upper and Lower Clapton Roads have become known as "Murder Mile" due to the high crime rate, mostly drug related, Sadly streets I used to walk as a schoolboy and as a young man have become 'no go' areas, especially at night.

The life of Jonathan Adams (1774-1842)

With the departure of brother John on the Bounty at the end of 1787, what had become of the younger Jonathan at the age of thirteen, both parents dead and seemingly no other close family?

On leaving the workhouse, an apprenticeship to a master would normally be arranged for the orphan children, sometimes for a fee, and therefore relieving the parish of the burden of further support. This would usually be for a period of seven years with the apprentice receiving no wages, but having all needs supplied by the master.

In Jonathan's case there is no record of him at the workhouse after 1783 and is mentioned again only at Deptford on the Bounty in 1787 saying farewell to John and after that, his eventual securing of an apprenticeship 'in 1789. As mentioned previously, it may be the 'intervening years were spent at sea or some other occupation.

What is known is that Jonathan somehow secured an apprenticeship at the age of fifteen with a Master Waterman by the name of James Brown from Aldgate,on the edge of the City of London.

The City as opposed to the city of London is usually defined by the ancient boundary walls, formally encompassing almost 450 acres, including the Tower of London and St. Paul's Cathedral, and many parish churches with the River Thames to the south.

Any businesses deemed to be undesirable, such as glue and soap making using fat and bones, gunpowder manufacture, tanning and dyeing of skins using urine and dog's faeces, along with prisons, lunatic asylums and unconsecrated graveyards, were all banished to outside the City limits. Access would have been through the ancient City gates that exist now in name only,such as Aldgate, Ludgate, Aldersgate, Cripplegate, Ludgate and Blshopsgate, all demolished by 1761.

The materials were sold off for new constructions and the widening of the London Bridge arches, with Newgate the last to go in 1777. The City area remains to this day the British and international financial capital still within the Roman 'square mile'. So in 1789 Jonathan Adams, after spending most of his young life in the rustic countryside of Hackney in the late 18th century, began his apprenticeship 'in the hustle and bustle of the capital where Samuel Johnson [1709-1784] stated:- that 'when a man is tired of London he is tired of life'. Probably true 'in his fortunate circumstances but for many

Londoners it was a daily struggle to exist. Jonathan's master, James Brown would supply board and lodging and training in the trade of Thames Waterman in return for assistance over a seven-year period. A rule laid down in the reign of King George II [1727-1760] states 'no waterman on the Thames shall take on an apprentice or servant unless he be an housekeeper or have some known habitation, and shall register the same with the clerk of the company on pain of £10.

Apprentices are not to take upon them the care of any boat 'till 16 years of age, etc. except that they have worked with some able waterman for two years at least, under the penalty of 10 shillings.'

The apprentice would have no income and would not be allowed to marry until completion of his apprenticeship, become licensed and achieved his 'freedom.'

Jonathan Adams was qualified after 7 years in 1796.

Aldgate, site of one of the original entrances to the old walled city of London from the east, is not actually by the River Thames. It is about a mile distant, north, from the tower of London so I think it is safe to assume James Brown's plying place would not have been far east or west of the Tower.

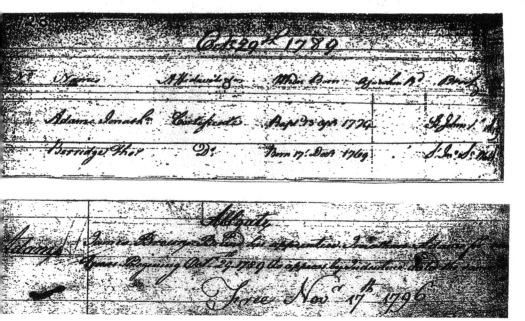

Freedom certificate after seven years' apprenticeship

Jonathan Adams was badge No. 2719
Courtesy of Docklands Ancestors

Crossing the Thames

Since ancient times, the River Thames running through the heart of London from its docks and quays has been a link to the open sea and a means to transport goods and people quicker and more easier than by the inadequate road system. By the 18th century, London had become the busiest and largest port in the world, trading with its far-flung empire and other nations across the globe.

John Burns [1858-1943], the historian and firebrand member of Parliament for Battersea is quoted as saying:- 'The St. Lawrence is mere water, the Missouri muddy water but the Thames is liquid history.'

For many years, unregulated crafts and watermen would ferry passengers up,down or across the river, but it was felt after several acts over the centuries to make the boats and passengers safe with a responsible owner, an Act to form a Company of Watermen was needed.

This came about in 1566 to put a stop to 'divers and many misfortunes and mischances, caused by evil and ignorant persons who robbed and spoiled of their passengers' goods, and also drowned them'. The Company was thus able to regulate its members and also look after their financial interests. Printed tables of fares were available every year from the early 18th century. Statutes and rules were laid down early on such as 'Waterman's names shall be registered by the Overseers and identified by a numbered armband corresponding to the number on their craft. Their boats or wherries must be twelve foot and half long and four and a half foot broad in the midship or be liable to forfeiture; and two men shall not ply but where one of them hath exercised the profession two years and been allowed by the overseers. Watermen taking more than the rates or fares appointed shall forfeit 40 shillings and suffer half a year's imprisonment; and refusing to carry persons for their fare, be twelve months.'

'Forty watermen appointed by the rulers are to carry passengers across the river on Sundays and being paid for their labour, the overplus money is to be applied to poor decayed watermen, etc. Where persons travel on a Sunday with boats they are to be allowed by Justice of the Peace, on pain of forfeiting 5 shillings, for every offence.

The Rose in June ~ a Thames Wherry
A reconstruction of a waterman's boat. Details were taken from
an apprentice's model dated 1781 in the Science Museum.
Built by Mark Edwards at Richmond.

*Extract from the 1808 Rhinebeck Panorama,
courtesy of the Museum of London.*

*The picture shows assorted craft in the congested Pool of London
below London bridge. To the west upstream is Blackfriars Bridge
with Southwark on the South bank.*

Before 1750 and the building of Westminster Bridge, the only means of crossing the river on foot or by carriage were the ancient congested and narrow London Bridge and distant Putney Bridge, and also the horse ferry that ran from the south bank at Lambeth.

Travelling through the many arches beneath old London Bridge by boat was seen as an extremely hazardous exercise but one that had to be constantly undertaken by the watermen. The increase in water flow through the narrow openings, originally nineteen arches, was a risky business and known as 'shooting the bridge.' The houses shown in old prints along the bridge were removed by 1762 and the two central arches replaced by a single span, and further needed support was added using stone from the demolished City of London gates. Up till the Restoration of Charles II it was a common sight to see the heads of traitors displayed on the bridge, serving no doubt as a deterrent in those uncertain times.

It was said that London Bridge was made for wise men to pass over and fools to pass under. An interesting speculation about Old London Bridge is that it could be the origin of why, in the United Kingdom, we drive on the left hand side of the road.

Due to its narrowness and the constant haphazard flow of traffic wishing to cross the Thames, congestion and delay was inevitable. Apparently, in 1722,the City of London brought in a regulation that to enable coaches, carts etc to pass one another in some sort of order, traffic from the south i.e Southwark were to keep to the west [left] side of the bridge and those from the City to keep to the east, thus keeping two orderly lines each keeping to their own left hand side. The idea must have been successful as the idea soon spread further afield and became accepted. One reason the left may have been chosen is that the walking public would be in less danger from a driver's whip. Another long held theory is that a right-handed man could more easily draw a weapon, if necessary, to confront someone approaching on his right.

New London Bridge

A new bridge design with just five stone arches, after rejection of a single span type, was one of 600ft. by Thomas Telford, but was not to be completed until 1831 almost at the end of Jonathan Adams' time on the river. This in turn was replaced in 1972 and sold to the Americans, legend saying they thought they had bought the more attractive Tower Bridge. Tunnels running beneath the Thames were to be a much later feature, starting with Marc Brunel's innovative Thames Tunnel between Wapping and Rotherhithe, at a cost of many lives, mainly due to pollution, through seepage from the river, and was dogged by a shortage of funds. Originally intended to be used by vehicles, the lack of money to finish the necessary work saw it remain as a pedestrian tunnel after its opening in 1843 until the 1860's. It is now used as part of the London Underground system. A long forgotten subway tunnel opened in 1870 between Tower Hill and Tooley Street in Bermondsey was a forerunner to the London Tube. With a diameter of just seven feet, although just a short journey it must have been quite claustrophobic for the passengers in the cable cars, paying for 1st class 2d and 2nd class 1d. It was later used as a foot tunnel, but when Tower Bridge opened in 1894 it became obsolete, and is now used for cables and pipes, although the round tower entrance remains opposite the Tower of London main entrance. Two more tunnels for vehicular traffic, Blackwall and Rotherhithe, and further east the pedestrian Greenwich tunnel, were built at the end of the 19th century and the early part of the 20th century.

After many years of debate and objections from the City Corporation and watermen but because of the increasing demand, a new bridge was finally completed at Westminster in 1750. No dogs were allowed on it and anyone found defacing the walls was threatened with death without benefit of clergy. Substantial compensations were paid to the Archbishop of Canterbury, owner of the horse ferry and to the watermen for loss of trade. The horse ferry was still in use in the 19th century and the name lives on in Horseferry Road SW1.

Watermen

Watermen and lightermen had existed separately since Elizabethan times but joined together to form the Company of Watermen and Lightermen in 1700 and responsible, in a highly regulated trade, for moving people and goods cheaply and safely anywhere between Gravesend and Windsor [later Teddington] at fixed rates.

In the reign of Elizabeth there was said to be up to 40,000 watermen making a living on the River Thames. Due to the rigours of the job it attracted hardy, tough individuals and coarse in their language.

When their behaviour got too bad, fines were issued with the funds going to the widows and orphans or less able bodied of the Company. It's not surprising when they had to work in all weathers on a polluted and hazardous river, which sometimes would be frozen solid for weeks. From the mid 14th century until early in the 19th century England was in the grip of a mini 'ice age' with especially severe winters. The first known Frost Fair took place in the early 1600s, although the river had frozen many times in the past. The Thames, at this time, was very polluted,more widespread and shallower during this cold period with little in the way of embankments, and a reduced flow from the damming effect caused by the many pillars of old London Bridge. For the short time the ice was thick enough Londoners would hold a Frost Fair and flock onto the ice to enjoy horse and coach racing, bull baiting, puppet plays, ox roasting as well as skating and sledding and general merriment. An elephant was known to have been led across the ice below Blackfriars Bridge. The enterprising watermen not able to do their normal job, made channels between banks and ice and charged to ferry revellers across. With the building of the new bridges, particularly London Bridge in 1831, much improving the water flow and the end of the mini ice age, the frozen river and the fairs became a thing of the past.

Watermen were used to ferry passengers at rates set by the company along both banks of the Thames, from dedicated plying places, known as 'stairs,' as they invariably led from street level down to the height of the tide. The craft or wherries used were to be of a good standard, registered and numbered, as were the owners or operators, with an armband, and boats to be regularly inspected. Apart from ferrying just ordinary passengers, watermen were also called upon to handle the fine craft of many dignitaries, including the monarch and members of the Royal Family, to reach palaces such as Hampton Court and Greenwich. Watermen were also employed for many state occasions, funerals and festivals. The men involved would usually be fortunate to have some protection from impressments by the 'press gangs.' Jonathan Adams was not to gain his protection until 1803, seven years after achieving his 'freedom' from apprenticeship, but not as a waterman but as a retained fireman. This may explain some of his missing years. More of which later.

With the various ways of crossing the Thames by tunnels and bridges and the arrival of steam boats and the improvement of roads, by the beginning of the 20th century, the trades of watermen and lightermen had diminished but not entirely died out. Lightermen for a while were much in demand, unloading shipping out in the river, onto their barges or lighters into the docks, making the ships lighter, hence the name. They were to become more of a feature of my ancestors employment in the mid 19th century, but with the opening of the London Docks lightermen were not so much in demand as the work was done by land-based 'dockers.' Containerisation from the mid 20th century led to the closing of the London docks with the new dock down river at Tilbury.

A Thames waterman at the opening of the new London Bridge in 1831. He is wearing the uniform of a Dogget's Coat and Badge winner, an annual race for apprentices just after achieving their 'freedom.' By Grant Osman. Courtesy of Docklands Ancestors

Frost fair on the Thames in 1814, looking east towards London Bridge. Courtesy of the Museum of London.

Jonathan Adams' marriage

A year after becoming a fully-fledged waterman, the parish records of St. John, Wapping in 1797 shows a baptism entry for an Andrew Steadman Adams, son of Jonathan Adams, waterman and his wife Margaret. Assuming a wedding had taken place sometime after finishing his apprenticeship and before the birth of his first child, I scoured local parish records starting with the nearest, St. Botolph's without Aldgate, for a marriage entry for the happy couple but with no result.

Aldgate, where he served his time is only a short walking distance to Wapping so I presumed, unless Margaret was from somewhere outside the immediate area, they must have married in a church not too far distant. My first guess however should have been the correct one but for unknown reasons it proved to be elsewhere.

Searching the parishes around Aldgate, Whitechapel, Wapping and the City revealed nothing and so I broadened the search to cover all the East End churches over a period of time, but frustratingly again no result. This raised the question of whether they were actually married at the time of Andrew's birth or had married against the terms of his employment during his apprenticeship, although I had allowed to a certain extent for that in my searches. As a last resort, as Jonathan was a waterman, I decided to try south of the river, although knowing that East Enders rarely ventured there even during my youth. In the late 18th century with no easy free crossing, apart from old London Bridge, it must have been a real barrier not just for people on the Middlesex side [North] but also the Surrey side [South]. So I was not hopeful, but as a waterman Jonathan Adams at least had access to a boat. So began the search of churches of Bermondsey, Deptford and Rotherhithe.

Naturally, I should have started directly opposite Jonathan's plying place, now at Union Stairs Wapping, where can be seen across the Thames the fine old church of St. Mary's Rotherhithe, but instead I worked from east to west. However, I finally found eventually what I was looking for at St. Mary's with a marriage between a Jonathan Adams and Margaret Mouncey in 1794. The question is, why there, when her home parish church of St. Botolph's-without-Aldgate was nearer and perfectly suitable? Further investigation now I had

Margaret's surname revealed that she was born in Aldgate and had a sizeable family living there. At the time of her wedding she was not yet sixteen years old and was probably marrying without her parents consent also Jonathan was breaking the terms of his apprenticeship. The witnesses on the marriage certificate don't appear to be relations of Jonathan or for Margaret, which leads me to believe it was a clandestine wedding. Did they believe she was pregnant though no records show this?

Jonathan Adams' marriage to Margaret Mouncey.
St Mary's, Rotherhithe 1794

The Mouncey Family

Margaret Adams, formerly Mouncey, was from the parish of St Botolph's-without-Aldgate, as indeed were many of her family as proved by a search through the parish archives. As Jonathan served his apprenticeship with his Master James Brown in Aldgate, it is assumed that he attended St Botolph's and must have become known to the Mouncey family.

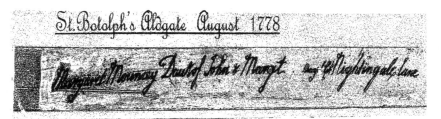

Margaret was baptised in St. Botolph's on 16th August 1778 and her marriage took place on 2nd June 1794 just short of her 16th birthday. Her family were from Angel Court and latterly Sun Yard, Nightingale Lane, just east of both the Tower of London and where later St. Katherine's dock was situated. The building of the dock in the 19th century in this area displaced thousands of residents to clear the site for the increasing need for storage and supply facilities and berths for the loading and unloading of ships. Nightingale Lane ran down to the river through the area known as East Smithfield, perhaps a byway used by Jonathan from Aldgate to his plying place as a waterman. Nightingale Lane is said to derive its name not from the songbird but from the boundary of the lands belonging to the Knighten Guild. This was a group of favoured knights in the 10th century, loyal to King Edgar who were rewarded with a gift of land at their request.

Margaret Mouncey's parents were John and Margaret and she had at least five siblings:- Sisters, Elizabeth born 1773, Amelia 1776, Sophia 1787, Ann 1789 and a brother Andrew Stedman Mouncey, 1791, later to become the uncle of Andrew Steadman Adams.

On further investigation the name Ste[a]dman seems to have been their mother's maiden name, used often as a middle name. The Stedman name also features frequently in the St. Botolph's parish registers as does the Adams surname, perhaps the reason Jonathan ended up in Aldgate, but that far back confirmation is difficult to prove from the basic information given.

St. Botolphs without Aldgate

St. Botolph's Aldgate is an old established church built around the 11th century and one of four built of the same name outside of the old City of London walls. Apart from Aldgate there was Aldersgate, Bishopsgate and, in 1666 destroyed in the Great Fire of London, Billingsgate.

St. Botolph is the patron saint of travellers and the churches were built for the spiritual wellbeing of people entering and leaving the City.

Daniel Defoe was married there in 1683 whilst working at the nearby Royal Mint. His description of the Great Plague in 1665 stated two pits dug in the churchyard contained 5,000 victims. Isaac Walton writer of the 'Compleat Angler' was also a parishioner.

In 1740 the church was declared unsafe by the surveyor Benjamin Franklin and was rebuilt at a cost of £15,500 in 1744, designed by George Dance, Clerk of the City Works.

There remains a fine Renatus Harris organ donated in 1676 by Thomas Whiting, a parishioner. It is probably the oldest church organ in the country, with its pipes in the original position on their wind chests.

During rebuilding, the body of a boy was found in a standing position in one of the vaults in a well preserved state, and people paid tuppence to have a peep and were most impressed with the condition of his intestines.

Literally a stone's throw from the Whitechapel murders of Jack the Ripper in 1888, the area the church stands on became known as Prostitute's Island, after being given immunity there by the police for their own protection.

St. Mary's, Rotherhithe

The church chosen by Jonathan and Margaret on the south bank of the River Thames has an interesting history. It lies amongst the disused warehouses, loft conversions and ever-increasing new riverside apartments in a small area of 18th century buildings and by an entrance to the engine house for Brunel's tunnel from Wapping, yet to be built at the time of their wedding. The tunnel was the first to be built under a waterway.

There has been a church on the site since the Middle Ages but, due to constant flooding was condemned by 17 10 but refused funding to rebuild by the Church Commissioners. After many difficulties the money was raised by the parishioners, mostly seafarers and watermen. A splendid new one was ready by 1715, believed to have been built by John James, a pupil of Sir Christopher Wren. The stone spire was added later in 1739. Some interesting interior features are the pillars made from ships masts covered in plaster. The Lady Chapel Altar and the Bishop's Chair are made of wood from a sailing ship from the time of Nelson, the 'Fighting Temeraire,' made famous in a Turner painting. The Captain of the 'Mayflower', Christopher Jones, lived for eight years in Rotherhithe and four of his children were baptised in St. Mary's. He is buried in the churchyard along with three other part-owners of the ship and are commemorated by a wall plaque. The 16th century pub next to the church,originally called The Shippe and later called the Spread Eagle and Crown, is now called the 'Mayflower' as Captain Jones moored his ship nearby. Apparently it is licensed to sell postage stamps, British and American. The crew of Jones' ship were mostly local men when the ship sailed from Rotherhithe, taking the puritan Pilgrim Fathers to set up a colony in America in 1620. After the Mayflower's return in 1621 and the death of Captain Jones in 1622, it was left to rot at the quayside before being sold for £120 to be broken up. It is believed some of the timbers were used in the church.

Another resident of the churchyard is the son of a cannibal chief, Prince Lee Boo, who when the East India sloop Antelope got in to difficulties off the Pelau islands in 1783, rescued the shipwrecked sailors. A grateful Captain Wilson, as a gesture of kindness, brought the 20 year-old Prince back to Rotherhithe where he died, unable to bear the English winter, at the Captain's house in Paradise Row. He is remembered in another wall plaque in St. Mary's.

So this was the church Jonathan and Margaret were married in. Why choose a church away from their own parish? The answers may be that Jonathan had still to finish his apprenticeship and strictly speaking was not supposed to marry until then. As for Margaret she had not quite reached sixteen, although girls could marry at twelve and boys at fourteen, but this had to be with parent's permission.

So not far in terms of distance from the home parish of St. Botolph's Aldgate just a short trip across the river, but if it was a secret wedding with no family members as witnesses, they were less likely to be known. From this unusual start the marriage was to last a good many years with several children and many descendants.

Church of St Botolph's-without-Aldgate

Church of St Mary's Rotherhithe

Naval Service

The marriage of Jonathan to Margaret Mouncey in 1794 produced their first child by 1797, after completion of Jonathan's apprenticeship the year before. Following Andrew Steadman Adams' birth it was to be six years before a second child was produced, namely John, my Gt. Grandfather [x3] in 1803, and siblings over shorter intervals afterwards. Could there have been a reason for this?

The years 1793-1802 were a time of great unrest in England after the French Revolution and the rise of Napoleon Bonaparte, with many of the British aristocracy dreading that the same could happen at home. The constant fear of invasion was another factor leading to the introduction of 'The Defence of the Realm Act' in 1798, brought in to recruit men for the Army and Navy. A strong navy has always been essential, as an island nation, to protect Britain's borders. To raise numbers from 45,000 to around 120,000 there were three ways to recruit sailors:- Volunteers, The Impress Service or the Quota Acts. The willing volunteers were obviously the most desirable recruits and indeed made up the backbone of the navy. The sailor would be paid a bounty and wages in advance to kit himself out.

In every port a 'Regulating Officer' would be a non-seagoing officer whose job entailed setting up a 'press gang', as the Impress Service would be known. His brief would be to recruit local hard men and ruffians, to trawl the ports and countryside to seize unwilling men between 18 and 55 but known to be seamen, although their suitability had a wide interpretation. A bounty would be paid for each capture, but corruption was rife and some unfortunate captives with enough cash could bribe their way out.

Once on board the ship the pressed men would be offered the chance to volunteer and would enter the ships muster book as such and receive the bounty plus wages, but never knowing when they might if ever return.

William Pitt brought in two Quota Acts in 1795, which stated each county according to its size of population and number of ports should supply a set quota of men for service at sea. Very few volunteers were forthcoming and sot he option was given to petty criminals to go to sea or go to jail. Many trivial offenders were given harsh sentences, including transportation and death and so, instead, some chose the maritime life. One drawback was many criminal recruits carried infections, such as typhus and gaol fever, not ideal to take aboard an otherwise healthy ship.

Many watermen, ideal recruits voluntary or otherwise, would form part of the Royal Navy during this time of crisis. Crew lists for ordinary seaman at this time are not usually traceable, especially without a name for the ships served in. Jonathan Adams could have been one of the patriotic volunteers or 'pressganged', as his immunity papers were not issued until 1803 and may account for the six-year period between sons Andrew and John being born.

A much longer gap than between each of the following four children. At the beginning of the 19th century there was to be a brief respite in hostilities between the British and the French, with both sides tired of war and Britain anxious to continue trading with the empire and so a peace treaty was signed in 1802, but only lasted just over a year.

By the next round of fighting in 1803, Jonathan almost thirty and the father of two sons may have been exempted from serving his King and Country,perhaps already having served, but sought immunity anyway and it was granted not for his everyday job as a waterman but as a newly acquired extra undertaking as a retained fireman for the London Assurance.

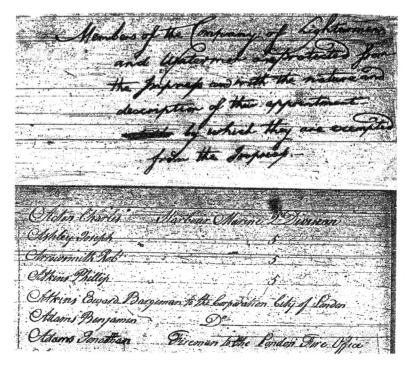

List of men protected from the press gang, 1803

One piece of irony if Jonathan was press ganged is that another name at this time for the Royal Navy was the 'Andrew', the same name as his young son. Named after an infamous leader of a Portsmouth press gang called Andrew Miller, his victims were said to be snatched by 'the Andrew' and so became a slang term for the Navy.

London Firemen

With the dawn of the nineteenth century, Jonathan after thirteen years must have assumed his brother John had perished, as no sightings had occurred of the mutineers and had probably given up hope of his return. Life went on for Jonathan living in Knight's Court, Wapping and working from his waterman's plying place at nearby Union Stairs on the north bank of the River Thames. The year 1803 was to be significant for him as it was the year his second child John [my Gt. Grandfather x3] was born, probably named after his long lost brother and deceased father. Also it was the year of his appointment to the part-time post of retained fireman with the added bonus that this would exclude him from the press gang. Once employed in this capacity he would be issued with an exemption certificate to always have about him, with a badge worn for identification.

After the Great Fire of London in 1666, to avoid a repeat of the disaster, regulations for the rebuilding of the City led to houses being built of brick, not too close together or overhanging, as fire was an ever present danger. From 1680 the first beginnings of an insurance fire service called the Fire Office, followed by many other insurance companies, was set up to attend only to fires on property covered by them. It was felt fire insurance companies, each with its own brigade were needed with a more organised and responsible system of tackling fires with the equipment to do the job. It was soon realised that rather than using casual labour, often men just there to pilfer, a dedicated and responsible band of firemen was required.

By 1720 it was seen to be an inducement to potential customers if an insurance company had its own brigade, and so it became essential for the insurers to employ their own firemen, supplied with an elaborate uniform, as a form of advertising. Almost exclusively in the London dockland area, the recruits for this lucrative part-time job were watermen known for their toughness, used to danger, quick-witted and normally known where to be found if summoned. There was no lack of recruits for this sought after job giving a supplementary source of income whilst still carrying out their waterman's duties.

Daniel Defoe states in his 'Essay upon Projects' commenting on insurance offices in 1697 that:

"If any fire happen they have a set of lusty fellows, generally watermen, very active and diligent in helping to put out fire". In his 'Tour through Britain' in 1724 he writes "The several ensurance offices have each of them a certain sett of men, who they keep in constant pay and who they furnish with tools proper for the work, and to whom they give jack-caps of leather, able to keep them from hurt, if brick or timber, or anything of not too great a bulk, should fall upon them; these men make it their business to be ready at call, all hours and night or day, to assist in case of fire; and it must be acknowledged, they are very dextrous, bold, diligent and successful. These they call firemen, but with an odd kind of contradiction in the title, for they are really most of them watermen".

A company would consist of between eight to thirty men for each brigade, the maximum allowed per brigade for impressment exemption, and some men to act as bonded porters to salvage goods in danger of being consumed by the fire. Brigades were commanded by a foreman who was sometimes on a salary,while the ordinary firemen would receive a retaining fee and paid for attendance to a fire or a drill with a fixed amount of money.

As free watermen, a large numbered badge identifying the man and his craft had to be worn at all times on the left arm. In the case of a waterman working for nobility or royalty a coat of arms on a silver badge might be worn. As a fireman the insurance company armband would also be worn with a distinctive livery supplied. Top hats were supplied by some companies for ceremonial occasions.

Although the livery was very smart and looked very good on parades it was not altogether practical for fighting fires. A petition presented to the London Assurance directors in 1763 by the porters and firemen of the company complained that the black shoes with silver buckles and leggings worn were no protection 'as their leggs are frequently torn with nails, barrs of iron and such kinds of rubbish as fires occasion'. The request was to have suitable boots supplied, for as well as protecting the legs the firemen were often working in difficult conditions in hot and cold water and was a cause of men taken ill afterwards. Later pictures show men wearing boots.

A story in the History of the British Fire Service by G.V. Blackstone states that a fire coat was worn on Pitcairn Island assumed to have belonged to one of the Bounty mutineers when press-ganged. This was unlikely as they were all volunteers. The coat, it is said, was used as ceremonial dress many years later. I think the only likelihood of that is if many years later Jonathan, after contact had been made, had the means to send one of his old coats to brother John, but this is the only reference I have found to this interesting item. The London Assurance, mainly involved in marine insurance, was the company Jonathan Adams joined and was issued with 'The Instructions for the Firemen' dated 1752, giving a comprehensive set of rules to their employees.

> *"They must get to the fire with their engine in the quickest possible time. They must obey all directions and orders of their foreman and if he be not present, of their deputy foreman.*
>
> *Every fireman must report to his foreman on arrival at the fire.*
>
> *He must be properly dressed and wearing his badge and number.*
>
> *He must be careful of the insured's property and cause no unnecessary damage.*
>
> *He must behave himself courteously and with diligence and fidelity and shall not ask for any reward from any sufferer nor favour any person for reward, promise or threat in securing his house, preferable to another but apply himself for the security of that which is most exposed to danger. The foreman or deputy shall take his axe and badge from any fireman that in drink or otherwise behaves rudely, negligently or disorderly, and deliver him into the office with an account of such behaviour.*

Footnote:- The above orders, rules and regulations are to be observed by all parties concerned upon pain of being cashiered. And every fireman is to give his place of abode in writing to be stuck up in the watch house, in order to be called on occasion.' During the 18th century a fee of one shilling would be paid for the first hour and sixpence for each subsequent hour. On being summoned by messenger and before attending to the fire first it would have to be ascertained that the property was insured by the attending brigade's company. This would usually be confirmed by the 'firemark', a plaque made of metal, usually lead or copper, and so likely to survive a fire. It was placed at high level to prevent it being stolen, at the front of the property and supplied by the relevant insurance company on payment of their premium. If found to be a house insured by another company the attending firemen returned to their station or hung around to jeer at rival crews. Although rare, firemarks can still be found today on walls in London.

London Assurance Firemark [1720-1965]
Britannia's shield bears the arms of the City of London and she holds an Irish harp above the policy number for the property.

London Assurance Fireman. 18th century.

BAGGAGE INSURANCE
IN 1730

'September 16th, 1730. £3,300 @ 30/-% His Excellency Horatio Walpole, Esq., on his Goods, Plate, Baggage and other Effects in the Middleton (Francis Pemberton, Master) from Rouen to Clye in Norfolk.'

In 1730, only ten years after The London Assurance was founded, annual Marine premiums already totalled over £25,000—and Horace Walpole's uncle chose The London Assurance to protect his goods on their cross-Channel journey.

Today, The London Assurance Marine premiums total well over £6,000,000, which shows the continued growth and vitality of the Company.

After nearly 250 years The London Assurance still holds a leading position in the insurance market for Marine—Fire—Life and Accident business.

 **THE LONDON ASSURANCE**

1 KING WILLIAM STREET, LONDON, E.C.4

"Very good people to deal with"

The London Assurance was founded as a marine assurance company but extended to include life and fire assurance, home and abroad.

106

This then was the service Jonathan Adams applied to join when attending a Court meeting at the London Assurance on the 30th March 1803.

The original document read as follows:

> *Then pursuant to the order of the day the court proceeded to re election of two firemen to this Corporation in the room of William Green resigned and John Medcalf dec'd and John Hesketh, Jonathan Adams, John Lipscombe and John Free were severall balloted for, and on casting up the Ballots it appeared that John Hesketh had 23 Ayes and no Noe, Jonathan Adams 23 Ayes and 1 Noes, John Lipscombe 5 Ayes and 19 Noes and John Free 4 Ayes and 20 Noes, so that John Hesketh and Jonathan Adams were elected in giving the usual securities.*

So began the double career, as waterman and fireman, of Jonathan Adams for many years to come.

John Adams adapted from a sketch by Capt. F.W. Beechey

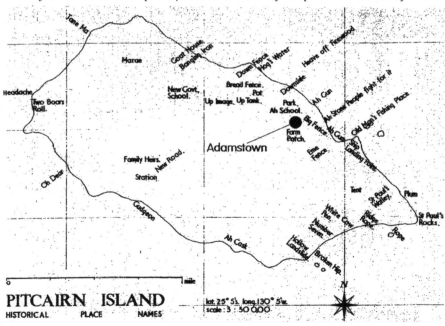

Map of Pitcairn Island
Courtesy of David Ransom. Pitcairn Island Study
Group.

108

Life and Death on Pitcairn Island

By the beginning of the 19ᵗʰ century, John Adams had survived on Pitcairn Island for over 10 years and seen many changes. Still unvisited by passing ships their feeling of isolation must have been complete.

The choice of refuge was fortunate as the island, although difficult to land on and only one mile by two miles, was fertile with abundant wildlife and sufficient fresh water.

The Bounty, soon after arrival, was stripped of everything useful and destroyed to avoid detection from passing ships. Their secret location was well kept as it was to be 19 years before another ship arrived in 1808. At the turn of the century the only surviving adult males were Ned Young and John Adams. Of the original nine mutineers and six Tahitian native men only these two were able to stay alive after much infighting over drink and the lack of female partners.

During the early years there was much bloodshed, fuelled by drink, mainly over the shortage of women. At the beginning, each mutineer had his own 'wife' from amongst the twelve Tahitian females, but perhaps not ones they had originally formed relationships with on Tahiti. This left the Tahitian men to share and as some women died they were expected to give up their women to the mutineers, leading to much resentment and unrest. Within two years of settling on Pitcairn Island two of the 'wives' died, one from disease and another from a fall whilst collecting bird's eggs on the rocky cliffs. The seeds of discontent had already been sown by the treatment of the Tahitian men with the unequal division of land. Originally they were seen as friends but then later treated as slaves, and were now told to forfeit their female companionship.

An overthrow of the white men was conspired but was revealed to them by the women, and two of the native men had to flee to the mountain area. In return for sparing the lives of the Tahitians left behind, the mutineers sent them to hunt down and kill the two fugitives.

After the deaths of these first settlers it was to be two years, during which time several children were born, before trouble flared up again. Although outnumbered, the natives once again set about trying to kill the white men when the women and children were out of the village collecting bird's eggs and swimming. The mutineers, on a fine day, were tending their plots and carrying out their chores.

John Williams was the first to be killed, shot by a gun borrowed on the pretence of shooting a wild pig. Fletcher Christian was the next to fall, followed by John Mills, Isaac Martin and William Brown. John Adams was the next to be shot in the shoulder and neck. In fending off the rifle he broke a finger and the gun misfired twice allowing him to run off into the forest. Adams was offered a truce and was re-united with Ned Young, believed to have known of the forthcoming trouble probably from the women with whom he was very popular. As a friend Young may have asked for John Adams to be spared and had been shot by mistake.

Quintal and McKoy had fled to the forest during the turmoil but the balance was now more even, with four white men and four natives and ten women. Even with the excess of women the natives could not agree on partners and arguments and fights broke out amongst themselves. Within a short space of time one Tahitian killed another and fled to the forest to join Quintal and McKoy. As part of a truce agreement, the two mutineers killed their fellow fugitive and returned to the village. With the two remaining Tahitian men the women took a hand in their deaths, killing one with an axe. The other lured by one of the women to show him the dead body, gave Young the chance to shoot the last remaining Tahitian man.

So, after barely four years, in 1794 on Pitcairn, eleven murders had taken place leaving just four mutineers and ten women and an increasing number of children. Relative calm was brought to the island now, for a time, with consideration given to the building of houses, cultivation of crops, fishing and the trapping of wild hogs.

Some of the women, homesick, and tired of living away from their families and friends, were discontented and wished to leave the island, even building a boat which never got underway.

Part of the dissatisfaction was caused by their bad treatment at the hands of Quintal and McKoy. This led to a couple of revolts but, when the men became aware of the conspiracy, threats were made to kill the persons responsible. The men were kept on their guard until the crisis passed and eventually forgave the women.

The behaviour of Quintal and McKoy can probably be explained by the latter's ability, after eight years, to make alcohol from the roots of the Ti- tree and sugar cane, distilling it in the Bounty kettle, a kind of all purpose cooking pot.

There followed a period of permanent drunkenness and wild

behaviour by Quintal and McKoy, leading McKoy to tie a boulder around his neck in a fit of depression and to throw himself off a cliff. Matthew Quintal was also becoming dangerously unstable and out of control, demanding another wife after Sarah died, and threatened another mother to kill her children if she would not live with him. A decision was made by Adams and Young, the only other remaining white men, to kill him. Inviting him for drinks, they waited until he was intoxicated and killed him with an axe.

Young was himself dying by this time from a lung disease. He was believed to be an educated man and before he passed away in 1800 he sought to improve the literacy of John Adams, principally using the Bounty Bible and Prayer Book. Adams may have already had some schooling in the workhouse and now the responsibility fell to him to pass his knowledge on to the next generation.

When Edward [Ned] Young died, Adams, the last surviving adult male, was left with a colony of eleven women and twenty children. John Adams had consorted with several women on Tahiti but his four children were all born on Pitcairn Island. Vahineatua [Prudence] was the mother of the first three children, namely Dinah [1796], Rachel [1797], named after his sisters and Hannah [1799] possibly after the wife or daughter he deserted in Hackney, as speculated earlier. After Prudence's death in childbirth, he took up with Teio [Mary] who gave birth to his only son George [1804], perhaps named after the man whose naval service he had deserted, King George III. The descendants of George Adams today are many and mostly spread around the southern hemisphere.

After the death of Ned Young, John Adams spent his days drinking a potent distilled spirit and intensively studying the bible. The result of this was an hallucination appearing of the Archangel Gabriel attacking him with a dart. So shaken was he by the vision that it transformed him overnight and he became deeply religious and so led to the saving of his small community and its moral welfare. John Adams, a man from humble stock, a semi-literate sailor, now set about educating the many children as a teacher and religious instructor and was now looked upon as their patriarch.

By the time of the first arrival of a ship in 1808, after nearly twenty years of isolation, Pitcairn had become a pious and model community, working for the common good. An American whaler the 'Topaz', under Captain Folger was the first to call, by chance, en route home from Hobart, not knowing Pitcairn was inhabited The American crew must have been amazed to find an Englishman with the same name as their second President of a few years earlier, who was also a founder member of their new republic.

Once Adams realised it was an American ship and not interested in taking him back to England he was relaxed and eager for news of the old country. He was informed of the rise of Napoleon and the wars between England and France and Nelson's victory at Trafalgar. As an old sailor this news greatly cheered him, throwing his hat in the air and shouting "Old England for ever." Captain Folger informed the Admiralty of Adams' whereabouts in 1809 but by then the Royal Navy were more concerned with a resurgent Napoleon than with capturing a mutineer missing for over twenty years.

Life on Pitcairn Island carried on, with its centre now called Adamstown and settled to routine of farming, raising hogs and chickens, fishing and recreations such as surfing in the dangerous water around the coast.

Jonathan Adams in Wapping

Apart from the baptisms and marriages of his children, there are some other incidences of Jonathan in records due to his occupation in two highly regulated occupations. One such regular mention is in the Quarterage payments paid as a subscription to Waterman's Hall for his licence to work as a waterman. As the name implies, this was paid three monthly on days with some names rarely used today such as Lady Day [25th March, start of the New Year before 1752], Midsummer Day [24th June], Michaelmas [29th September] and Christmas Day [25th December].

One curious event on record is an incident where he is falsely accused of rowdy behaviour. This comes from an article in the Times newspaper on the 12/9/1831 under the heading 'The Watermen and the Steamers'. These vessels powered by steam, carrying many passengers, were used for daily excursions to places such as Margate from the centre of the capital, beginning around the 1820s. The steamship operators had an uneasy alliance with the watermen. It seems with the arrival of a steam vessel, the 'William Fawcett', one Sunday off Bermondsey on the River Thames there was 'an unseemly scramble for fares taking place by several watermen' causing chaos and confusion. Ignoring the byelaw that just two boats should be alongside at any one time, large numbers were crowding round the steamer. The ensuing disorder led to passengers being separated from their luggage, left on either bank, and the commander of the steamer fearing someone would be drowned.

Asked by the magistrate if any watermen could be identified, the commander stated that he had taken the numbers of the most offensive. Waterman's Hall later identified one of the offenders, number 2719, as belonging to Jonathan Adams. However, Adams was able to prove he was not alongside the steamer at the time and it appeared his number was misread or was used by another. The magistrate asked for the culprits using other watermen's numbers to be tracked down.

The commander of the steamer did not wish for anyone to be issued with a £5 fine but just for the incidents to stop. After this, further disembarking was monitored by the Thames River Police, perhaps by Jonathan's son John, from the nearby Wapping Police Station.

Present day site of Jonathan Adams' last plying place

Jonathan Adams' admission for a pension aged 59
(25th June 1833)

By 1833 and approaching sixty, in a physically demanding job, Jonathan Adams was qualified for retirement with a pension of 10 shillings a week. His last plying place was Wapping New Stairs, adjacent to Wapping Police Station and the so called 'Execution Dock.' Stow is quoted as describing the dock as:-'The usual place for the hanging of pirates and sea rovers at the low watermark and there to remain until three tides had flowed over them.' The bodies were sometimes taken from there in chains down river to Bugsby's Hole, Blackwall, hung from a gibbet, and left on display to rot as a deterrent to ship's crews entering London.

By the time of the first census in 1841, Jonathan is a widower still living in Knight's Court after over 40 years, with his eldest daughter Mary and her three children. Mary's husband John Berry is not shown, so presumably as a mariner he was away at sea. This was the first and last time Jonathan Adams appeared in a census, as he died at home the following year of dropsy, after a full life and at a good age for that time of sixty-eight.

1841 census, Knight's Court, Wapping
Jonathan Adams, widower, living with his daughter Mary's family.
Husband, John Berry, a mariner, not present, probably at sea.

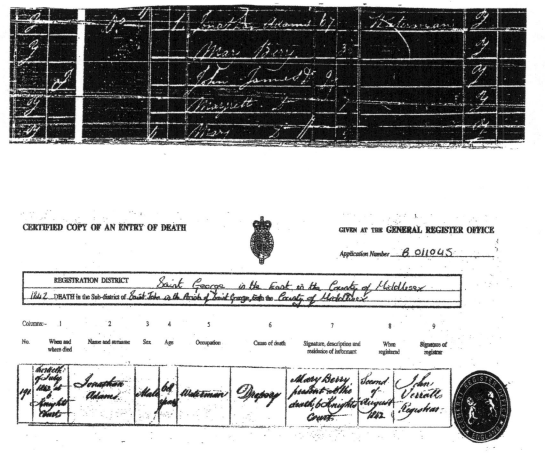

Death certificate for Jonathan Adams, Knight's Court, Wapping, 1842

Pitcairn in the 19th century

Entering the new century, John Adams found himself the only European and adult male and patriarch to his flock of women and children. The days were gone now when he was known as Reckless Jack and discipline and hard work was essential for the colony to survive indefinitely. Fortunately, there was an abundance of food on the island as crops such as yams, taro, coconuts, breadfruit and figs were readily available, as was freshwater. Goats, pigs and fowls were plentiful and fish caught in the surrounding sea.

By the time Captain Folger of the 'Topaz' arrived in 1808 he commented that he found 'the world's most perfect and pious community' and the people were "athletic, tall, robust, golden limbed and good natured of countenance"It is a great irony that an infamous act and so much bloodshed and violence could result in a peace loving community, working for the common good, and must be to the credit of John Adams. Day to day life on Pitcairn carried on in its mundane way with Adams doing his best to educate and instil Christian virtues into the children. The routine would be broken only over the years after the visit of the Topaz, by passing ships bringing news of the outside world, of which only John Adams had any real knowledge of.The visits were welcomed by John Adams now he felt secure from capture and he let it be known what his real name was.

By 1823 many ships had visited but none bringing family or friends and so Adams, now fifty-six, resigned himself never to see kith or kin again. This was the year the British whaler 'Cyrus' arrived bringing the first non-mutineer or non-Polynesian to settle on Pitcairn. John Buffet was an educated man and accepted by Adams, as old age came upon him, to act as a schoolteacher. Buffet was given permission by the Captain of the 'Cyrus' to leave the ship but another sailor by the name of John Evans jumped ship and hid away until she sailed. Both men were to marry before long, Buffet to Ned Young's daughter and Evans to John Adams' daughter Rachel. John Adams himself was officially married to his long-time partner Teio,now blind, by Captain Beechey of the 'Blossom' in 1826. After over 30 years on Pitcairn, John Adams revealed his fears to Captain Beechey of the island becoming overcrowded now that the children had grown up, married and having children of their own, expanding the population. He secured a promise from Beechey to seek help from the British Government for another larger island where they could settle, develop and cultivate the land. Captain Beechey was true to his word but John Adams died on 5th March 1829, aged sixty two, before his wishes could be carried out. His blind wife Teio died nine days later.

JOHN ADAMS'S GRAVE, PITCAIRN.

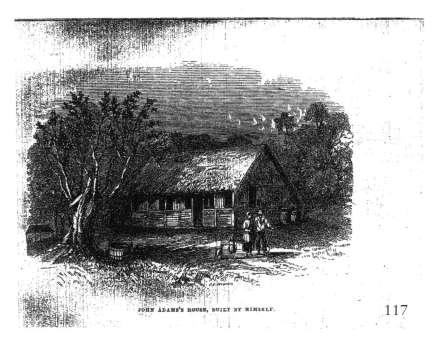

JOHN ADAMS'S HOUSE, BUILT BY HIMSELF.

Pitcairn's Church and School

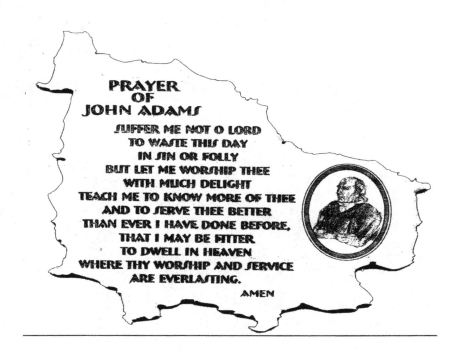

PRAYER
OF
JOHN ADAMS

SUFFER ME NOT O LORD
TO WASTE THIS DAY
IN SIN OR FOLLY
BUT LET ME WORSHIP THEE
WITH MUCH DELIGHT
TEACH ME TO KNOW MORE OF THEE
AND TO SERVE THEE BETTER
THAN EVER I HAVE DONE BEFORE,
THAT I MAY BE FITTER
TO DWELL IN HEAVEN
WHERE THY WORSHIP AND SERVICE
ARE EVERLASTING.

AMEN

Return to Tahiti

Following on from Beechey's request, a decision was made, probably with the best intentions but was to end in disaster, to transfer the Pitcairners, in 1831, to Tahiti the home of their forefathers.

Now numbering eighty seven people with an average age of seventeen, they embarked on the 'Lucy Ann,' escorted by HMS Comet and set off for Papeete in Tahiti. On arrival, the pious Pitcairners were shocked by the licentious behaviour of the natives, coarsened and diseased by the visiting Europeans, vastly changed from the pure and innocent natives of Cook's time.

Before long many of the immigrant Pitcairners succumbed to a terrible fever, and showing little resistance twelve of their number died, After five months on Tahiti and losing another five people they were allowed to return to Pitcairn Island. They were fortunate to arrive when they did as the empty island was just about to be annexed by the French. They also found everything in disarray, believed to have been caused by natives from Bora Bora. No other attempts were made to relocate until 1855 when with the population nearing two hundred, no fish in the sea having moved elsewhere, and food generally becoming scarce the question arose again about resettlement.

A letter was sent to Queen Victoria requesting help and in a generous offer, Norfolk Island in between Australia and New Zealand was offered. Newly abandoned, the ex-penal colony was almost empty and no longer used after the transportation of British criminals was stopped. This was to prove ideal, being much bigger with a moderate climate. After some initial hesitation by a few of the Pitcairners, perhaps remembering the move to Tahiti twenty years before, on the 3rd May 1856 they set sail on the 'Morayshire' for their new home on Norfolk Island 3700 miles away. However within five years forty-four people unable to settle on Norfolk Island returned to Pitcairn Island [the population today is still around fifty] but the majority stayed, including all the Adams descendants where they remain to this day.

Jonathan Adams' children

After Jonathan's marriage to Margaret in 1796, he was to live the rest of his life in Wapping, firstly in Upper Gun Alley and later in Knight's Court. His first born son, Andrew was baptised in the local church of St. John's, Wapping in 1797. The tower of the church survives today, although damaged in WWII, and is now the centre of an apartment block.

By the turn of the century, and for the next forty years, his home in Knight's Court a small alley off Tench St, was just a short walk from his plying place, originally believed to be Union Stairs but by 1800 Wapping New Stairs. Following a gap of six years, possibly serving his country, his second son John, my Gt. Grandfather [x3] was born in 1803 with other siblings at short intervals, all baptised at the main church for the area St. George in the East.

St George in the East

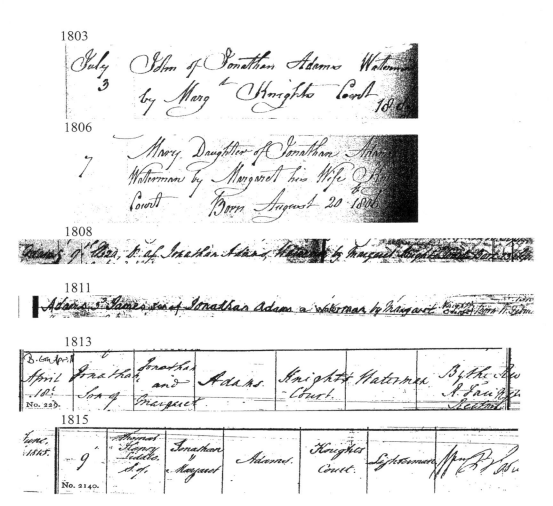

Baptisms St George-in-the-East

Mary, his first daughter, was born in 1806, Eliza in 1808, James in 1811 and Jonathan Jnr. in 1813. There is also a recorded baptism in 1815 at St. George in the East of a Thomas Henry Liddle Adams, parents Jonathan and Margaret Adams. The use of the three forenames and father's occupation is curious which doesn't seem to fit in to the rest of the family and so perhaps Thomas was taken into the family after some tragic circumstance or an illegitimate grandson. No more is yet known of the fate of Thomas Henry.

Traditionally, a Master Waterman would apprentice his sons in the father's trade, not least because under the rules of apprenticeship he would have to support the boy for seven years. One advantage of this is that as a son he would still be living at home anyway. The records at Waterman's Hall show that all four sons, apart from the mysterious Thomas Henry, were apprenticed to their father, but only John was to complete the required number of years and achieve his 'freedom' in 1826.

At the baptism of Andrew Stedman Adams and wife Amy's daughter Louisa in 1817 he is shown as a waterman but is unlikely to have been licensed. James Adams and wife Ann, at the baptism of their daughter Margaret Grace in 1836, shows his job to be a labourer.

Brother Jonathan Junior went on to join the newly formed London Fire Brigade, now replacing the various insurance company brigades, in 1832, probably influenced by his father's many years as a retained fireman with the London Assurance.

Eldest daughter Mary, who was to stay close to her father for the rest of his life was married to John Berry, a mariner from Leith in Edinburgh at St. Mary's church, Whitechapel in 1829.

Daughter Eliza was married to Peter Hales in 1828. {Died in the Whitechapel cholera outbreak, along with her daughter Eliza Ann, aged 18 months, in 1833}.

John Adams, my Gt. Grandfather [x3] served his apprenticeship between September 1818 and January 1826.

However, three months after achieving his 'freedom' he decided to join the Marine Police Unit based in Wapping, said to be the oldest organised Police Force in the world brought about to combat the high level of crime associated with the river traffic and docks. His retirement documents state that in 1856 he was unfit for further service after serving thirty years and that he was eligible for a pension of £39 per annum.

He is mentioned in several transcripts of trials at the Old Bailey as the arresting officer and witness. The Wapping police station punishment book has entries for minor transgressions, such as being absent from his post and for twice attending court whilst off duty and improperly interfering in cases. He obviously wanted to see justice done but was reprimanded the first time and both reprimanded and suspended on the second occasion. His pension was probably not enough to live on and at the age of 53 he needed another source of income.

By the time of the 1861 census he turns up as a Tower Liberty Beadle. The area of the liberties were set up originally as protection around the Tower of London but mostly were left unoccupied towards the end of the 17th century. Over time, encroachment and redevelopment took place, so to protect the areas Liberty status was applied for and granted. These became autonomous areas, leaving its citizens free from jury service at county courts and assizes and to run its own affairs and rarely having to pay rates.

Tower Liberty would have its own prison and courthouse situated in John Adams time in Wellclose Square and he would have assisted in keeping law and order within its limits, as well as on vestry business. After the middle of the 19th century the power of the Liberties was gradually eroded.

Mary Adams, wife of retired police officer and beadle John Adams, died in 1862 of Bright's Disease aged sixty-one. John Adams died in Mile End Old Town, aged sixty-six, of paralysis and apoplexy in 1870. His son, Francis Jonathan Adams, my Gt. Grandfather [x2], the notorious 'Bluebeard' and possible Jack the Ripper suspect, died in Tooting in 1918, aged seventy-six, of senile decay.

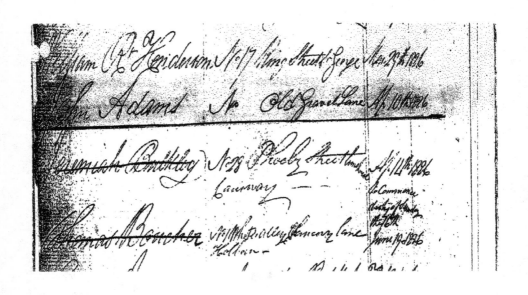

John Adams finishes his waterman's apprenticeship after seven years on 8th of January 1826 and joins the Thames River Police in Wapping on 10th April 1826.

Norfolk Island Resettlement

On the 8th June 1856 the 'Morayshire' landed 193 persons on Norfolk Island, comprised of just eight Pitcairn families. Amongst these were the children and grandchildren of the Bounty mutineers Adams, Christian, Young, Quintal and McCoy. Amazingly, for a group of people brought up on a tiny island there was no suggestion of in-breeding or genetic faults. It is believed that the Tahitian women were well aware of the dangers and prevented it from happening.

The journey of almost 4,000 miles had taken five uncomfortable weeks, with much sea-sickness arriving on the anniversary of the Bounty's commissioning nearly seventy years before.

The new residents of Norfolk Island [pronounced Nor-folk by the locals] were supplied with enough food, grain and livestock to enable them to establish themselves until their own crops were ready. Most of the convicts had already left but some that remained helped the settlers to learn new skills, such as sheep shearing, milking and tending the crops in the fertile soil.

The sea surrounding the island with an abundance of fish was another important source of food. Passing whaling ships would also employ men, and at one time whales were frequent visitors to Norfolk's shores. Eventually, the islanders set up their own whaling industry, which lasted until 1962 by which time stocks had diminished.

Many things were unfamiliar to some Pitcairners on their arrival, and a wonder, having never seen horses and cattle or houses made of stone, left by the former residents of the penal colony.

Having left Pitcairn, the new arrivals were under the misapprehension that Norfolk Island would be theirs to do with as they wished, as they had on Pitcairn. However, the British government had other ideas and insisted the coastline and common roadways could not be owned. The situation of wishing to be autonomous from any mother country still exists today. Although Great Britain gave up all rights to Norfolk Island in 1914 it is governed now by Australia.

The land was fairly portioned out and so began the building of a flourishing community, which today numbers around 2,000, with plenty of mutineers descendants names still to be found, so many that to differentiate between some of the same name, nicknames are often used.

With its year-round good climate, history and tax-free status, Norfolk Island is sustained by its tourist industry served by its international airport.

Of the twenty five men accused of the mutiny on the 'Bounty,' John Adams was to outlive them all, creating his own dynasty through his only son George whose many descendants today are centred on Norfolk Island but can also be found around the world. George had three sons by Polly Young:- John b. 1827, Jonathan b. 1829, and Josiah b. 1830 who between them had over thirty surviving children to perpetuate the Adams line in their new settlement. George died in 1873 aged sixty-nine on Norfolk Island.

Adams' Reunion

As the inevitable consequence of many years of research of the London side of the Adams family tree, I felt I needed to know more about the Norfolk Island branch. Researchers of the Bounty and John Adams have known for some time of the existence of a brother named Jonathan but had little information as to his fate once the two had gone their separate ways.

I corresponded by e-mail with the historians on Norfolk Island but it seemed I was the first to come forward with any details of the mutineer's brother. I was put in touch with Boyd Adams, a resident of Norfolk Island and a direct descendant of John Adams, who sent his family tree but again no information on my Gt. Grandfather Jonathan Adams. A meeting was arranged when Boyd arrived on a trip around Europe in 2002. The venue arranged, which I thought would be appropriate, was at the Prospect of Whitby in Wapping. On the appointed day Boyd and his cousin Jacqui, living at the time in France, and their partners arrived. Introductions were made, followed by lengthy conversations about our lives and the local history.

This meeting was the first between the two sides of the Adams family since 1787 when John and Jonathan bade farewell to each other at Deptford on the deck of the Bounty, not realising the separation would last two hundred and fifteen years.

A walk around historic Wapping was next, the area frequented by our forefathers, pointing out various places of interest. Although severely altered during the building of the docks and bombing during the Blitz there is still plenty to show how things used to be when it was 'Sailortown' with taverns every few yards. Jonathan Adams was to walk the streets of Wapping for fifty years and the area must surely have been visited by his brother John before sailing on the Bounty.

It was a brief meeting as they had to continue on their journey but were resolved to stay in contact and perhaps meet again some time in the future.

Alan and Boyd Adams outside St. John's Church, Wapping

Norfolk Island Visit

In 2005 as part of a trip to Australia, along with my brother and nephew and their partners, we made the short trip to Norfolk Island. The, visit was planned to coincide with the annual 8th June Bounty Day anniversary when the first landing in 1856 is recreated. Once the small rowboat has landed a service is carried out at the memorial, then a walk to the cemetery followed by hymn-singing and celebrations.

The ceremony and festivities afterwards were rather spoiled by the unusually foul weather but it was still a moving occasion.

We met up again with Boyd Adams and received a cordial but low-key welcome from some of the other members of the family, some Quintals and the curator of the island museum.

Norfolk is quite a small place and nowhere is more than twenty minutes away and so during our week there, although a good experience, we found the island to be too isolated and limited.

I think that Norfolk Island is a nice place to visit with a good climate,interesting history and a laid back lifestyle but it would not suit everybody. On balance, I'm glad Jonathan Adams stayed in London and created the basis for future generations of which I am a part. We Londoners are the product of survivors of the fittest, our ancestors overcoming war, disease and poverty and lived to create the great and endlessly fascinating city that London is today.

Norfolk Island

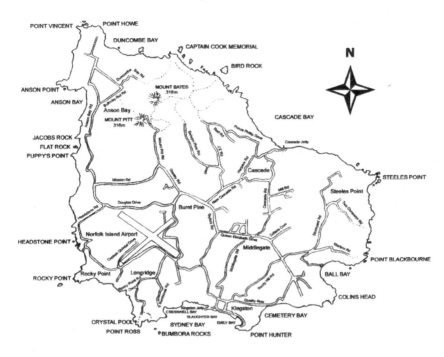

Emily Bay on Norfolk Island

*Annual Bounty Day
Celebration 8th June*

Conclusions – London

By the 1870s with the deaths of my Gt. Grandfather [x3] John, the son of Jonathan, in Wapping and John's only son George, on Norfolk Island, each side of the family were living entirely different existences. Jonathan's descendants, from his son John, to eke out a living in the Dickensian conditions of Victorian London as part of a large family in the squalid and poverty stricken East End.

With the construction of the London Docks vast residential areas were swept away, making many people homeless. The jobs for watermen now were few as more bridges were built, but increased work was to be found around the docklands area, loading and unloading ships on the busy River Thames. My side of the Adams family was headed from 1870 by the philanderer and the father of at least twelve children by four women, Francis Jonathan Adams. The first two 'wives' died young, including my Gt. Grandmother from his first recorded marriage, the third one he deserted before embarking on his second and last recorded marriage as far as is known at the present time.

During the next forty years we were to begin to gradually head back north, eventually back to Hackney where my earliest records start. Around 1850 Stepney, just a short walk from Wapping was to be the family home until moving to Spitalfields, then the Mile End Old Town area and finally by 1900 to Bethnal Green. Regarded at the time as a poor, run-down area the old properties, survivors of the Second World War, are now much sought after. This is probably due to the proximity to the City and even the Sunday flower market has a middle class feel to it. We were to stay there until I was seven years old when our house in Columbia Road, no bathroom, and toilet at the end of the garden, was demolished as part of a slum clearance in 1953 and we moved to Hackney.

So after the enforced move to Hackney the circle was now complete with the family's return, although unknown to me before my search began. The roads trodden by my generation, and those in the 18th century, such as from Stamford Hill through Clapton to Mare St. [formerly Church St.], Hackney had been country paths two hundred and fifty years before, but some still follow the same lines today between Bethnal Green and Stamford Hill.

My school, Upton House in Homerton, actually overlooked both the old and the newer St. John at Hackney churches and perhaps if I realised the wealth of history at that time I may have discovered all that I have set down, sooner.